George Maloney

God's Community of Love

Living in the Indwelling Trinity

New City Press

Dedicated to
Cindy and Bill Murphy
who bring a smile to my heart whenever we meet.

Sincere thanks to
Sr. Mary Faith, O.S.B., June Culver
and Frances Phelan for their help.

New City Press, 202 Cardinal Rd., Hyde Park, NY 12538
©1993, George Maloney
Printed in the United States of America

Cover art by Doris Gmür

Imprimi Potest:
Bert R. Thelen, S.J.
Provincial Superior, Wisconsin Province

Library of Congress Cataloging-in-Publication Data:

Maloney, George A., 1924-
    God's community of love : living in the indwelling
Trinity / George Maloney.

    Includes bibliographical references.
    ISBN 1-56548-042-2 : $8.95
    1. Christian Life—1960- 2. Trinity. I. Title.
BT111.2.M25   1993
231'.044—dc20   92-42031

First published in February 1993 as *Be Filled with the Fullness of God*
2d printing: August 1995

Bible quotations are from *The Jerusalem Bible*
©1966 Darton, Longman & Todd, Ltd. and Doubleday & Co., Inc.

Contents

Introduction

Batter my heart, three-personed God, for you
As yet but knock, breathe, shine and seek to mend;
That I may rise, and stand, o'erthrow me, and bend
Your force, to break, blow, burn and make me new.
I, like an usurped town, to another due,
Labor to admit you, but oh! to no end;
Reason, your viceroy in me, me should defend,
But is captived and proves weak or untrue.
Yet dearly I love you, and would be loved fain,
But am betrothed to your enemy.
Divorce me, untie, or break that knot again.
Take us to you, imprison me, for I
Except you enthrall me, never shall be free;
Nor even chaste, except you ravish me.

John Donne

In this poem the poet, John Donne, writes profoundly of the truth that all of us human beings some time on our earthly journey should become utterly convinced of: ". . . for I except you enthrall me, never shall be free; Nor even chaste, except you ravish me." Only if God ravish us shall we be what God created us to be.

The great revelation Jesus came to give us was to reveal to us that God is an ecstatic, intimate, loving community, a circle of inflaming love that knows no circumference, of a Father emptying himself into his Son through his Spirit of love. Such intimacy and self-emptying are returned by the Son gifting himself back to the Father through the same Spirit. In the Trinity, Jesus reveals to us the secret of life. Love is a call to receive one's being in the intimate self-surrendering of the other. In the ecstasy of "standing outside" of oneself and becoming available through the gift of love to live for the other, the Father and the Son and the Holy Spirit all come into their unique being as distinct yet united persons.

An emptying love

God's pursuing love for us, his readiness to forget and empty himself completely in order to fill us with himself as gift, is seen in his "pathetic" or suffering love, revealed and manifested to us in human terms in Jesus crucified. Nowhere has God's love reached a greater peak of fiery heat and self-giving to us than in the image of Jesus on the cross, totally broken, rejected and poured out for love of us. We can whisper in shuddering faith, as Paul did, that he "loved me and sacrificed himself for my sake" (Ga 2:20).

Gazing upon Jesus on the cross, the image of the invisible God (Col 1:15), we know now something of "the breadth and the length, the height and the depth" (Eph 3:18) of the love of Christ and of the Trinity that will always be beyond all human knowledge (Eph 3:19). Now the experience of such infinite, ecstatic love of God for us, made manifest for us in the human form of the suffering and dying Jesus, we can be "filled with the utter fullness of God" (Eph 3:19).

Living in the indwelling Trinity

The secret of our continued growth in prayer and the Christian spiritual journey is one of growing in greater and greater degrees of awareness and conscious experience of God's immanent or indwelling presence as self-emptying love within us. How truly sad that Jesus Christ, God's living Word made flesh, and still revealing to us the mysteries of God through the gift of his Holy Spirit, wishes to lead us into the presence of the Holy Trinity as the source and ultimate center of all reality, and, we in general remain ignorant of this truth.

For most of us Christians, the reality of the indwelling Trinity within us and permeating all of creation as the reason why all creatures live and move and have their being (Ac 17:28) is lightly dismissed as a mystery. We feel a supernatural mystery is something beyond our knowledge and understanding. Therefore, it can have no "practical" impact on our daily lives. It simply is a mystery!

I come to give you life

I often ask myself, "What would Jesus say if he were to reappear in human form and experience the level of Christian life preached and lived by modern Christians in their church-communities, homes and market-places?" He surely would find Christians who worship a loving God on Sunday and yet who do not love each other. Christian leaders of the Catholic, Orthodox and Protestant Churches profess with their parishioners in their ancient creeds their faith in the all-loving Trinity, and yet fail to bring such an intellectual assent to this revealed truth into their daily living experiences.

I believe Jesus Christ would ask each of us this fundamental question: "What ever happened to my revelation about my Father and me coming to dwell in you through our Spirit of love?" Would he not complain that the life he came to bring us has become diluted, a drop of water, taken from a torrential waterfall, and placed in a stopped up test-tube? "I came to give you life, that you might have it more abundantly" (Jn 10:10).

This life is to be an ongoing process of knowing and loving, of experiencing profoundly the Father and the Son in the Spirit, dwelling and actively emptying themselves in their unique personhood within us out of their burning, perfect, humble, self-sacrificing love.

Scope of this book

I have sought in this book to highlight God's purpose in creating us that we may share, even now, in his very own family, trinitarian life. God's revelation through Jesus Christ teaches us that we can both "know" and experience this mystery of the indwelling Trinity in us. As Christians we are all called to this. We are all called to experience this indwelling trinitarian life which transforms us into beautiful, loving children of God and brothers and sisters to all other human beings in Christ and his Spirit of love.

Relying on the writings of scripture, the mystical theologians of both Eastern and Western Christian theology and the mystics of all ages, I explore in the initial four chapters what we can learn about the eternal triune community within its inner circle of a unity in one nature of three distinct persons. These inter-trinitarian relationships are seen as the basis for God's essential relationships to us and the created world.

The remaining five chapters deal with the loving relationships of the "three-personed" God in their created world, especially toward us human beings, made in God's very own image and likeness (Gn 1:26-27). God is an involving God who wants to get closer to us, not merely by giving us material gifts of creation, but ultimately he must want to share divine personhood with us. God wishes not just to communicate ideas about his divine nature to us, but to be in intimate *communion*, ecstatic union, with each of us.

The Trinity is *primal grace* as the self-giving of each unique person of Father, Son and Holy Spirit to us in the uncreated energies that bombard, penetrate, surround us at every moment in and through each creature. We see these personalized energies of God working in our lives by discussing how we are divinized into becoming really loving children (1 Jn 3:1) and made participators of God's very own nature (2 P 1:4). This process of divinization is continuously taking place by Jesus Christ as he dwells within us and through the transforming love of the indwelling Spirit.

We conclude this book by reflecting on the Holy Trinity in the eucharist. By eating the body and drinking the blood of Jesus Christ, we also partake of the entire Trinity. Nowhere on earth or in heaven do we more powerfully encounter the family of God, the Trinity, than in the eucharist. The response of such a participation on our part as Christians is to go out in the power of this transforming, indwelling Trinity and celebrate the cosmic eucharist as we cooperate with the uncreated energies of the Trinity to build a better world.

Creation is not finished. The body of Christ has not been reconciled back to the Father through the Spirit of love within his members, you and me, and all other human beings living on this earth. The cosmic eucharist has not yet reached *communion*: men and women, united with each other as brothers and sisters of Jesus Christ and of the one heavenly

Father, human beings in peace and harmony with the sub-human cosmos, bringing it into fulfillment according to God's eternal plan.

If this book does not treat the mystery of the Trinity with perfect clarity and precision as other earlier books purposefully strove to do, I ask the indulgence of the reader. This book has been my humble attempt to see a different approach to this central mystery of the Trinity and God's humble, outpoured love through the indwelling within us as personalized Father, Son and Holy Spirit. This approach we find in the gospel, in the early patristic tradition when theologians were thinkers, but also mystics, who were taught by the same indwelling Trinity as they were purified of their own images of God and allowed the Spirit to reveal what is given only to the "pure of heart."

If you, reader, have been stirred to experience with greater awareness the indwelling Trinity as a "consuming fire" (Heb 12:29), who dwells within you as in God's very own temple, a house of prayer and worship, then my humble efforts will be greatly rewarded and the blessed Trinity greatly honored.

George A. Maloney, S.J.

Chapter 1

Loneliness Seeking
a Loving Community

Loneliness seeking a loving community

Newspapers reported that suicides among teenagers increased by forty percent in 1991. A new study showed 2.5 million men over forty years of age prefer their being single to marriage. One who represents the majority of such single men surveyed gave for his preferred state of being not married: "I have the freedom to make my own decisions without consultation. I just don't want to confer with anyone else, and I like that."[1]

We have been created by God, out of God's infinite love, to live, move, and have our being in God. Because we don't know where we came from or where we are going, we prowl about this earth seeking what we can devour, in our feverish hunt for happiness and self-fulfillment. We look for it in autonomy, money, possessions, travel, food, sex, and yet all things fail to feed the hunger in our hearts for a love that never ends, a happiness that never stales.

Made for love out of love

From the first time we wept as infants left alone by our mothers, we began learning that no one can be happy without love, without a loving community. By ourselves we are helpless, threatened, anxious—fragile as cut flowers. Without our roots deep in the common soil, touching the roots of others, we dry up and wither. Only by touching another in love do we know where we leave off and the mystery of the other begins. Only by love can we penetrate the mystery of God as the *ground* of our being and the mystery of our own uniqueness, beautiful self in his eternal love.

As babies raised without the touch of love pine and die, so do adults if they separate themselves from those who would love them and be loved by them. Aborigines, lying curled up together in their cold caves, perhaps understand more about our inborn need of closeness than do we, separate, self-centered, and lonely in our private bedrooms. The first loving touch of another human being is the beginning of our discovery of God, who is love (1 Jn 4:8), and points us toward the center of ourselves where God lives as a community of self-emptying love. When we find God there, we see that the other person is waiting for us, because God is at his or her center also.

The energy of God meets itself coming and going when two of God's children meet heart to heart, eye to eye, mouth to mouth, in an exchange of life and breath, close as the Trinity itself, loving and being loved in an endless circle of light and warmth, like the slow, timeless whirl of galaxies spinning through each other in space. That eternal, divine love that moved the sun and other stars precipitated the Word, Jesus Christ. He became enfleshed as a human man so that we could, by knowing and loving him, be gathered up in the arms of God the Spirit, out of the swaddling clothes of our flesh.

Our crave for intimacy

All around us, especially in the Western, industrialized countries today, we see a frenetic search for greater human fulfillment than what can be attained merely on the level of possessing more material things, seeking more sense pleasures or even developing a bonding among human beings into a more gentle society of a "thousand lights." It is fundamentally a search for God that lies at the heart of today's world crisis.

We crave intimacy with God as the source of our life and the goal of our inner yearnings. Yet, as we stretch out toward perfect, inexhaustible beauty, we find our hands closing into a tightness of a fist instead of an open hand toward Someone beyond us and yet living also invisibly within us.

We have polluted our interior environment. What we see around us in the pollution of air, the streams, rivers, lakes and oceans, our woods and forests and countryside, and in the jungles of our cities, is but an *icon,* a dramatic image, externalized, of what we human beings are doing within ourselves in the unlimited expanses of our inner space. There we were meant to run, fly, soar with the speed of light. No space, no time would hold us back as we were to be propelled into the future by the created energy of love, bubbling forth from the center of our being. Instead, we sit now, so lonely within ourselves, sick and afraid.

Julian Green puts it succinctly: "God is dying of coldness. He knocks on all the doors, but who ever opens? The room is taken. By whom? By ourselves."[2]

A personalistic, triune community

No doubt the impersonalism of our technological world has made us the center of our desires. How can we move away from finding our identity in ourselves as isolated, lonely individuals, possessing many things, find our true unique personhood beyond the perishable, in God's intimate community of love?

We crave to become "persons" also through our dissatisfaction with our Christian religion, especially through the teachers who have so often presented to us a God as separated from his immanent, creative, energizing love in all of his material creation. Even when preachers speak about God in personalistic terms as "he" or the Father, Son and Holy Spirit, all too often the three persons of the Trinity are presented as three "objects" to whom we are to address all our needs.

How can we enter into a Christian spirituality that presents God in personalistic terms of a loving community of three persons, Father, Son and Holy Spirit, sharing their unique self-giving to us as different persons in a unifying, one nature that is eternal love? We will show in succeeding chapters how the divine Trinity is inserted into God's created world. But we must begin to deepen our Christian spiritual life by experiencing the essence of God as oneness and yet threeness, a community of self-emptying love for each of us by turning into the mystery of God's identity within the Trinity as three persons in oneness of nature through God's revelation in scripture.

A revealed mystery

The mystery of the Trinity has been revealed to us in holy scripture. Revelation is a communication from God to us, made in his own image and likeness (Gn 1:26-27). It is a manifestation of truths revealed by God who makes them known to us through the incarnate Word of God that God-Trinity reveals the true nature of the inner community of God, Father, Son and Holy Spirit. We cannot know the inner nature of God unless it be revealed through God communicating this truth through his Word, Jesus Christ, and his Spirit. As Irenaeus in the second century stated: "For by the hands of the Father, that is, by the Son and the Holy Spirit, man, and not merely a part of man, was made in the likeness of God."[3]

Jesus Christ came to give us the most important truth upon which all of reality is founded. He came to teach us that we are unique persons, not by being an isolated individual, but by being in vital, loving and personal relationships with another person. But he came to make it possible by his Holy Spirit to know and experience this truth as grounded in the truth of God's intimate essence.

Jesus reveals that our most unique and meaningful personality, that empowers us to love God with our whole heart and love all other human beings as we love ourselves, can come only from the basic personalized community of love that is at the heart of the *I-thou* and *we* community of love, the Trinity of the Father, Son and Holy Spirit.

Let us now consider what God through the incarnate Word, Jesus Christ, and the Holy Spirit has revealed about the basic loving community, the Holy Trinity, that makes all other loving communities possible.

Notes

1. *Los Angeles Times*, 25 September, 1991, sec. E, 1.
2. Julian Green, *Journal;* Tomes 1-7 (Paris: Plon, 1928-58), 439.
3. Irenaeus, *Adversus Haereses*, vol. 6 in *The Ante-Nicene Fathers*, 1, ed. A. Roberts and J. Donaldson (Grand Rapids: Eerdmans, 1962), 531.

Chapter 2

Two Looks Devoured By Love

Two looks devoured by love

To enter into the very inner nature of God-Trinity, we need to move away from the limiting objective world of clear and distinct ideas to embrace an *apophatic,* mystical approach to the divine Trinity. Only such an approach will be a necessary corrective to prevent us from objectivizing God or the three persons into three distinct and separable Gods.

The apophatic theology of the Trinity is a unique characteristic of the early Eastern Fathers. For them *apophatic* is usually translated as negative, but this is to misunderstand the nuanced mysticism of these early mystics. The accent is entirely on God doing the revealing, giving the gift of himself. No longer is the emphasis on ourselves and our own personal thinking or praying activities. God, who is so infinitely perfect, good, beautiful and incomprehensible to our human mind, deigns to allow us to know him in some fashion or other by way of a direct experience built on the infusing of the Holy Spirit of faith, hope and love.

Vladimir Lossky well describes the apophatic approach of Eastern Christianity:

> The negative way of the knowledge of God is an ascendant undertaking of the mind that progressively eliminates all positive attributes of the object it wishes to attain, in order to culminate finally in a kind of apprehension by supreme ignorance of him who cannot be an object of knowledge. We can say that it is an intellectual experience of the mind's failure when confronted with something beyond the conceivable. In fact, consciousness of the failure of human understanding constitutes an element common to all that we can call *apophasis,* or negative theology, whether

16

this apophasis remains within the correspondence between our mind and the reality it wishes to attain, or whether it wishes to surpass the limits of understanding, imparting to the ignorance of what God is in his inaccessible nature the value of a mystical knowledge superior to the intellect.[1]

Love is a circular movement

Perhaps we can best enter into such a mystic vision of the inner relationships of the Trinity by viewing two different Christian art depictions of the Trinity. How many times have we seen in Roman Catholic churches the Trinity represented in the persons of a white-bearded Father, with his son holding a globe of the world and the Spirit as a dove hovering over both of them?[2]

In contrast to this Western approach to present in art the Trinity as three distinct (and separable!) persons, we offer one of the classics in Byzantine iconography, the icon of the Trinity, painted by the Russian monk, Andrei Rublev (c. 1408-25). He paints the three angels who appeared to Abraham at the oak of Mambre (Gn 18) to describe in art the revealed teaching of the one Godhead and the three persons in the Trinity.

The artist uses a circle as a basic form of composition, building a series of intersecting circles depicting the intimate relationships of the trinitarian persons, the Father, Son and Spirit, to each other. It is a mystical vision, that is meant to be contemplated in adoration and humility by the faithful of the inner trinitarian life of movement and rest, of peace and joy, of a community of three in a oneness. This community of unity in diversity constantly moves out from the Father to the Son under the loving gaze of the Spirit, depicted as the third angel, dressed in a green cloak, the sign of youth and fullness of powers, emanating from both the Father and the Son.

In this painting, there are no straight lines or angles; only a series of intersecting circles to catch up the viewer into the circular movement of the very life of the triune God that paradoxically reveals a distinction of persons, yet a oneness of nature. The three persons in peaceful repose express a movement of loving surrender toward each other in a stillness that hints at a loving communication of total self-giving in the power of silence.

Darkness within the Trinity

The early Eastern Fathers saw the Trinity as the source of all reality, the basic community of persons living for each other, begetting each other into his unique personhood by the self-emptying love that Jesus imaged when he appeared on the cross as a heart pierced and from which poured out blood and water. But before they speak of the heavenly Father within the Trinity, they begin with the *Godhead*. Before the Father can be a realized relationship toward the Son in the love of the Spirit, there exists the Godhead as the "unoriginated source," the principal root of unity in the Trinity. Meister Eckhart, the fourteenth century Dominican mystic of Rhineland, called this Godhead the abyss, the desert, the wilderness, prior to all movement toward other persons in loving relationships. This Godhead is "motionless unity and balanced stillness and is the source of all emanations."[3]

Godhead does not yet describe a personalized mind that speaks a personalized Word and thus becomes a mind by such a thinking-love action. There is in the Godhead fullness of being, but silence is what is before the Father hears himself speak his Word. Such indeterminateness is not negativity, or absence of being. It is the fullness of richness and is beyond all classification of being.

The Father begets his only-begotten Son

But out of this dark void of utter richness there stirs a movement "outward," toward another. The dark side of God's *no-thingness* turns to light as God wishes to find himself in self-giving to his Word. Thus, out of the darkness of unrealized potentiality in self-giving, the Father becomes Father and finds his true personhood in not only giving himself to his Son, but in himself being retrieved from non-beingness to being this Father of this Son.

Gregory of Nazianzen, the great fourth century Greek theologian, who wrote so eloquently about the Trinity, describes the Father as the source and goal of diversity or personal relationships within the Trinity:

> The nature is one in three; it is God; but that which makes the unity is the Father, from whom and to whom the order of persons runs its course, not in such a way that the nature is confused, but that it is possessed without distinction of time or of will or of power.[4]

Now God has a name, Father, because his meaningfulness is expressed in his self-giving to his Son through his Spirit of love. Two persons look at each other and are devoured by Love as they find their uniqueness as free, loving persons in living for the other. God would always have remained the void, infinite potentiality, had it not been through the stirring of the Spirit of love to call the Father out of the darkness into the light through his love given to and returned by his Son.

The I is the child of the We

Gabriel Marcel, the French Catholic philosopher, poet and playwright, gives us a most important principle in inter-personal relationships, that applies primarily to God-Trinity and secondarily to angelic and human persons who share in God's nature. He writes: "The *I* is the child of the *We*."[5] The Father as Father cannot exist in his essence as Father. He comes into his unique personhood as Father only in a loving "passing-over" beyond himself to be "birthed" into his unique I-ness in the Trinity by his self-emptying love toward his Son. This love moves him by the *kenotic* or hidden, self-emptying Love, the Holy Spirit, into the unity-in-diversity with his Son in the Spirit.

Many of the Eastern Fathers were fond of using the word, *ekstasis* (ecstasy), not as we understand the term, but in the primary meaning in Greek to mean the loving moving-out of the Father or the Son toward each other through the loving Holy Spirit. It is an habitual "standing outside" of one's controlled and self-possessing being. It is *availability* of the Father to be vulnerable, self-giving, to sacrifice himself joyously for the good and happiness of the Son and vice versa through the Spirit of love.

Now we know through Jesus Christ and his Spirit that not only is God one in nature, but also is a community or intimate family of loving persons who discover their uniqueness by living in self-sacrificing love for each other. God-Trinity is truly an *I-thou-we* community. It is an ecstatic, loving intimacy of a Father emptying himself into his Son through his Spirit of love. Such intimacy and self-emptying are returned by the Son gifting himself back to the Father through the same Spirit.

In the Trinity, Jesus reveals to us the secret of all reality and life itself. Love is a call to receive one's being in the intimate self-surrendering of the other. We can find full happiness and meaningfulness only in a community of love. It is only in inter-personal relationships based on self-sacrificing love as a free gift of oneself to the other and a return back to the first giver that God, Father, Son, Holy Spirit and all created intellectual beings can find each one's own unique personhood. Only such a person is free enough to love others with such agapic, self-emptying love as the Father and the Son have in their mutual Spirit of love for each other.

In the very self-giving of the Father to the Son and the Son to the Father a third person has his being. The Holy Spirit proceeds as the love between the Father and the Son. Each person is a presence of love to each other as gift, a giving away in free self-surrender of each to the other. And paradoxically it is also a receiving of new life, new openness, that yearns always more to live as gift to the other.

Love begets love

In summary we have seen how the unexpressed Godhead is beyond all being and hence all relationships. It is when God's nature as one moves toward self-giving that God takes on the personal relationship that is called Father to Son. This is God's holiness as he moves toward his Son to discover his being in knowing himself in his Son by begetting him in self-sacrificing Love, the Holy Spirit.

Before there is any exploding of this powerful implosive love between the Father and the Son through their mutual Spirit of love and the beginning of creation, all reality is already contained within the circle that has no circumference: the Trinity in its inter-personal relationships of Father, Son and Spirit. We human beings, with our limited intellects, can only receive a dim ray of light, a mere spark of fire as to the ecstatic, joyful love that passes from Father to Son as giver to receiver and back again as receiver from the Son—the giver—through the bonding of unity in uniqueness of persons, the Holy Spirit.

Revelation opens us up to the mystery all of us on our earthly journey seek to live out, namely, that true, self-sacrificing love is always a form of the dying and rising process. It is a losing of a lower level of consciousness only to gain a new-founded sense of uniqueness in the union in love with another. Love begets love, both in the giver and in the receiver. In the Trinity, the love of the Father for the Son in the Spirit calls out the uniqueness of the Son. Such a discovery of the Son's *thou-ness* in the Father's discovery of his unique *I-ness* in the Spirit begets in the Son his *I-ness* and the gift of himself as giver to the Father. The Father receives that gift of the Son in the same Spirit as Love.

The good news

The good news that Jesus Christ, as the full revelation of the Trinity's inter-relationships, gives to us through his Spirit is that the very trinitarian relationships within the Trinity explode outward as three persons in the one divine nature of love in creation wish humbly to share their joyful happiness and life, perfect beauty and power with us, made according to their own image and likeness (Gn 1:26).

In order to see how the Father and Son and Holy Spirit uniquely give themselves in loving action to us according to their unique, personal way of existing and acting toward each other in the Trinity, we need to reflect now on the uniqueness of the Son and the Holy Spirit within the Trinity and in creation. For the primal relationships within the Trinity give uniqueness of personhood to the different members of the Trinity. They are the basis for similar triune action toward a created world and toward us as predestined by God's gratuitous choice (Eph 1:4 ff) to become his children, participators in God's very own nature (2 P 1:4).

Notes

1. Vladimir Lossky, "Apophasis and Trinitarian Theology," *In the Image and Likeness of God* (New York: St. Vladimir's Seminary Press, 1974), 77-78.
2. Karl Rahner claims most Christians believe in tri-theism, three Gods, and not in the Trinity of three persons in one nature. Cf. *The Trinity* (New York: Herder & Herder, 1969), 10-11, 99.
3. *Meister Eckhart*, ed. Franz Pfeiffer, trans. C. de B. Evans (London: Watkins, 1947), 1:267.
4. Gregory of Nazianzen, *Homilia XLII* 15 (*PG* 36. 476).
5. Gabriel Marcel, *Metaphysical Journal*, trans. Bernard Wall (Chicago: H. Regnery Co., 1952), 26, 147, 221.

Chapter 3

The Father Begets the Son

The Father begets the Son

There are three characteristics of all true intimate love relationships, whether within the Trinity or between the Trinity and us human beings or between two loving human beings. These three basic characteristics of authentic, intimate love are *availability, mutuality and sacrificing of oneself* as a gift for the happiness of the other.

We human beings by God's plan are this way, hungering to find someone else to be always open, vulnerable, totally available as a loving presence, eager to share ourselves in a certain degree of equality on the greatest levels of human awareness on body, soul and spirit levels. We ever so slowly learn through our stubborn resistance to the truth that there can be no true love that will call us into our unique and beautiful personhood except that we and our loved ones are ready to die to any self-centeredness and be ready at all times in all circumstances to sacrifice oneself for the happiness of the other.

This is so among us human beings, only because this is the truth in the most primal community that constitutes all other realities as true and real in their existence, namely, the Holy Trinity. God's availability, as Jesus Christ has revealed this truth to us and the teaching of the Church has constantly affirmed it, is the Trinity's act by which the Father, Son and Holy Spirit are freely open as a loving presence to each other. They share themselves and their unique and different personhood with each other on all levels of conscious giving by self-forgetting and living to bring forth the other in unique beauty in and through the hidden, self-emptying love, the Holy Spirit.

God the Father speaks his Word in his Spirit

God the Father, in absolute silence, in a communication of love impossible for us human beings to understand, speaks his one eternal Word through his Spirit of love. In that one Word, the Father is perfectly present, totally available to his Son through the Spirit in sharing his complete being in total self-emptying. "In him lives the fullness of divinity" (Col 2:9).

The Word, having received his uniqueness through the eternal mind that utters his Word in love, the Spirit, turns back to his source and the Father hears his Word come back to him in a perfect, eternal yes of total surrendering love, that is again the Holy Spirit.

The Trinity is a reciprocal community of a self-emptying movement of the Spirit of love between the Father and Son in complete availability, mutuality and self-sacrificing on behalf of the fullness of the other. Our weak minds cannot fathom or imagine the peace and joy, the ecstasy and ardent excitement and exuberant self-surrender that flow in a reposeful motion between the Father and Son through the Holy Spirit. God within the Trinity becomes three persons in one nature, existing really only because the Father can lose himself in self-gift to the Son through the Spirit, only to find himself as unique and different, but still in loving union with the Son, always through the bonding Love, the Spirit.

Before we can understand how this trinitarian movement indwells us and sweeps us up into an unchanging, always freshly new action of divine self-giving in the deepest communion possible to us human beings, we must seek to understand what revelation has given us about the inner trinitarian life in the relationships that exist within the Trinity between the Father with his Son and Holy Spirit. For God must be consistently always the same. His mode of acting is his very unique personhood. Hence God the Father, Son and Holy Spirit act out of their unique personhood. God the Father, Son and Holy Spirit are distinctly different in personhood within the Trinity and also in and through the Trinity they act differently toward us human beings and toward all of God's material creation. God's acting and being within the Trinity as unique persons of Father and Son and Spirit must be the identical manner of their unique form of acting toward us in the created world out of the being of Father, Son and Spirit within the trinitarian relationships.

The cloud of unknowing

Whatever human words may be used to penetrate somewhat the inner mystery of God's nature as love in a communion of persons, our attitude demands something of the apophatic approach of the early Eastern Fathers and Christian mystics down through the centuries, who learned so well from scripture and from their own sense of brokenness in prayer that only God can lead us into this mystery. We must realize that we cannot comprehend God's inner life completely or we would have to be part of that Godly family by our very own nature.

Yet scripture insists that we can know this Trinity, but by a process of not knowing with our minds alone. In our poverty and utter creatureliness, even in our sinfulness and alienation from the Father, we realize, that to know God intimately and to dare even to imagine living a life of God's intimate, self-sacrificing love in total availability and mutuality in the greatest intimate union as children, made by God's grace participators of his own divine nature (2 P 1:4), lies beyond our own power.

"No one has ever seen God; it is the only Son, who is nearest to the Father's heart, who has made him known" (Jn 1:18). Yet we can come to know the Father through the revelation of the Son: "And eternal life is this: to know you, the only true God, and Jesus Christ who you have sent" (Jn 17:3).

As we Christians grow in contemplation of the indwelling Trinity, we realize more and more that God must reveal himself to us. We can only humbly wait in the desert of our nothingness, hoping to receive God as he wishes to make himself known to us. With the humility of children we seek entrance into the heart of God as he communicates himself to his Word through his Spirit of love. This is the teaching of Jesus, who speaks about the possibility of such children receiving, not merely knowledge or a communication, but the privilege in contemplation to enter into the very trinitarian "communion."

I bless you, Father Lord of heaven and of earth, for hiding these things from the learned and the clever and revealing them to mere children. . . . Everything has been entrusted to me by my Father; and no one knows the Son except the Father, just as no one knows the Father except the Son and those to whom the Son chooses to reveal him. (Mt 11:25-17)

The incomprehensible is made comprehensible

From the revealed word of God in the Old and New Testaments and in the living tradition of the Church through the centuries, the divine nature is considered as inaccessible, uncommunicable to us human beings. Etiénne Gilson well expresses this foundation stone for all of our human relationships with God:

Lower even if only for an instant and at one given point the abyss between God and man created by the contingency of creaturehood and you have taken away from the Christian mystic his God and hence his mysticism also. Any God who is not inaccessible, man can dispense with. It is the God who is by his nature inaccessible whom man cannot do without.[1]

Yet Jesus Christ promises us in the New Testament revelation that this inaccessible God with the individualized life of the trinitarian persons will descend and enter into our very beings. "If anyone loves me he will keep my word, and my Father will love him, and we shall come to him and make our home with him" (Jn 14:23).

Jesus Christ is the Word and the Son of the Father. He is the way, the truth and the life (Jn 14:6) that brings us into the awesome mystery of the Trinity as a communion in its own life.

The Word of God

The Word of God is found in scripture and in the Church's liturgical prayers as referring to the Second Person of the Trinity. The early

Eastern Fathers knew that any discussion of the inaccessible God and the immanent union with his creatures, his human children, must start with the divine *Logos,* the Word of God inside the Trinity. This is the *speech* of God in his divine, eternal existence that allows God to move in his spoken or pronounced Word outside of the inner trinitarian life in the created world.

The Gospel of John powerfully speaks of God's eternal Word in oneness of nature with God: "In the beginning was the Word: the Word was with God and the Word was God" (Jn 1:1). This divine Word became flesh and "pitched his tent among us" (Jn 1:14). It is he, therefore, who alone can reveal to us that the Father is known to himself and to us in and through his every Word. "He is known by the name, *The Word of God"* (Rv 19:13).

Ignatius of Antioch describes how God manifests himself through his Word: "There is one God, who manifested himself through Jesus Christ his Son, who is his Word proceeding from silence."[2]

This Word is the perfect image of the invisible God (Col 1:15). He is the thought of the Father that contains all the knowledge that the Father has of himself and of his eternal Son and of all things in that Word. "He is the radiant light of God's glory and the perfect copy of his nature" (Heb 1:3).

Everything comes from the Father

Scripture teaches us in the words of Jesus Christ that the Word of God receives all its force and power from the Father. He is the perfect reflection of the Mind that speaks this word.

> The Son can do nothing by himself; he can do only what he sees the Father doing: and whatever the Father does, the Son does too. (Jn 5:19)

Again Jesus says: "And my word is not my own: it is the word of the one who sent me" (Jn 14:24). He can do nothing of himself. The truth and judgment that he renders is that which the Father pours into him (Jn 5:30). He is light from light, true God from true God.

The Son of God

The term *Logos* had an appeal in the early Church for those educated in terms of Greek philosophy, such as Clement of Alexandria, Origen, Athanasius and the Cappadocian Fathers, Basil, Gregory Nazianzen and Gregory of Nyssa. But for the ordinary pious Christian this doctrine was too abstract and impersonal.

Thus the term *Son* was more frequently applied to Jesus Christ as the Second Person of the Trinity who became human to make it possible that we human beings might become divinized as children of God, living in intimate union with Jesus as the head of his body, the Church. John presents the Son as the expressed love in human form of the Father for us. "Yes, God loved the world so much that he gave his only Son so that everyone who believes in him may not be lost, but may have eternal life. For God sent his Son into the world . . . so that through him the world might be saved" (Jn 3:16-17; also 4:9).

The Godhead knows itself in its Logos, the perfect reflection of the eternal mind. But when the Word becomes flesh and dwells among us and reveals to us that God is a Father who gives himself completely in the begetting of his only-begotten Son, then you and I open ourselves to an experience of God in a new form of knowledge. God does more than know himself in his eternal image. But he empties himself in self-giving in total availability and mutual sharing of the same nature with his Son.

> For the Father, who is the source of life has made the Son the source of life. (Jn 5:26)

Of all the Old and New Testament writings, it is in John's gospel that we see most clearly the Father and Son relationship described to us. Jesus never links himself with us in a commonly shared sonship. He reveals to us that his sonship is unique, from all eternity, "I am ascending to my Father and your Father, to my God and your God" (Jn 20:17).

The only-begotten Son of the Father

John's gospel clearly brings to a fulfillment what was hinted at in the frequent use in the synoptic gospels of the title of "Son of Man." Twice in the prologue of John's gospel Jesus Christ is referred to as the "only Son" (*monogenes:* the only-begotten) of the eternal Father. This man, born of Mary, claims to exist before Abraham, when he uses the verb that Yahweh used to reveal his Godhead to Moses (Ex 3:14): "I tell you most solemnly, before Abraham ever was, I *Am*" (Jn 8:58). He is a person, who has come "from above" (Jn 8:23), ". . . the Son of Man who is a person, who is in heaven" (Jn 3:13). He speaks of what he has seen with "my Father" (Jn 8:38). And the Pharisees and scribes understood clearly his revelation and sought to stone him for seeking to make himself God (Jn 10:33). Clearly we know and believe the Father has a Son because he sent his Son into this world, not to judge, but to save it (Jn 3:17). Knowledge of the Son is as important as knowledge of the Father in order to obtain eternal life (Jn 17:3). The Son confesses that he is not independent of his Father, but that he depends totally upon him as his source of being (Jn 5:19-20; cf. Jn 6:57; 8:29; 12:49; 17:1 ff).

The Father is greater than the Son (Jn 14:28) since everything that the Son has comes to him from the Father as from his true and only source. Jesus is in the Father and the Father is in him (Jn 14:10). One has only to see Jesus and he or she sees the Father.

In the Johannine last supper discourse (Jn 14:17) we see an outpouring of the heart of Jesus as he reveals to us the intimate relationship he enjoys with the Father. The doctrine of grace as primarily uncreated energies of love poured out from one person to another in the hidden *kenotic* or self-emptying love of the Spirit would be developed from such a revelation. Thus we can readily understand how important it is to ground ourselves on this basic revelation of the Trinity from scripture in order to extend those intratrinitarian relationships into our own divine filiation with the Father through the Son in his Spirit.

Because of this New Testament revelation, we can believe with certain knowledge that the Father begets eternally his only-begotten Son through his Spirit of love. He gives him his very substance, not partially as in human generation, but his total being, all except his unique fatherhood which the Father receives only in vital relationship of "pass-over" love of complete self-emptying into the Son as the Son "others" the Father by calling him, Abba!

This faith, based on God's revealed Word made flesh, Jesus Christ, as found in the New Testament writings, has been formulated clearly in the profession of faith of the Council of Constantinople (381 A.D.):

> I believe in God, the Father Almighty,
> in one Lord, Jesus Christ,
> only Son of God,
> born of the Father before all ages,
> God of God, Light of Light,
> true God of true God,
> engendered, not created,
> of one substance with the Father.

Since the Son is one in substance with the Father, he, through the incarnation, cannot only bring us to a knowledge of the Father, but he can actualize ourselves through his Holy Spirit into children of God, sharing in his very own nature (2 P 1:4).

A most fitting conclusion of this chapter on the mystery of the Trinity's love for all of us through the Father's Son made flesh in order to effect the end of the incarnation expressed in the words of Athanasius, quoting Irenaeus: "For he was made man that we might be made God,"[3] are the beautiful, poetic words of Gregory Nazianzen in his twenty-ninth *Oration:*

> He was born,
>   but he was already begotten;
> He came forth from a woman,
>   and he kept her a virgin.
> He was wrapped in swaddling bands,
>   but he removed the swaddling clothes of the
>   grave when he rose from the dead.
> He was laid in a manger,
>   but he was glorified by angels,
>   and proclaimed by a star,
>   and worshiped by the wise Magi.
> He had no form of beauty in the eyes of his people,
>   but to David, he was fairer than all the children of men.

On the mountain, he was bright as the lightning.
    He became more luminous than the sun,
    illuminating us into the mysteries of the future.
He was baptized as a man;
    yet he remitted sins as God.
He was tempted as a man,
    but he conquered as God.
He suffered hunger,
    but he fed thousands.
He knew what it was like to thirst,
    but he cried: "If any man thirst,
    let him come to me and drink."
He experienced weariness,
    but he is the peace of all who are sorrowful
    and heavy-laden.
He prays,
    yet he also hears prayers.
He weeps,
    but puts an end to tears.
He asks where the lifeless Lazarus is laid,
    for he is a man;
and he raises Lazarus from the dead,
    for he is God.
As a sheep he is led to be slaughtered,
    but he is the Shepherd of Israel,
    and also of the entire world.
He is bruised and wounded,
    but he heals every disease and every infirmity.
He is lifted up and nailed to the tree,
    but by the tree of life he restores us.
He lays down his life,
    but he has the power to take it up again.
He dies,
    but he gives life, and by his death
    effectively destroys death.[4]

Notes

1. E. Gilson, *The Mystical Theology of St. Bernard* (New York: Sheed & Ward, 1940), 120.
2. Ignatius of Antioch, *Letter to the Magnesians* 8:2 (*PG* 5.765).
3. Athanasius, *De Incarnatione* 54 in *St. Athanasius: Select Works and Letters*, vol. 4, ed. Philip Schaff and Henry Wace, *A Select Library of Nicene and Post-Nicene Fathers of the Christian Church*, 2d Series (hereafter *LNPF*) (Grand Rapids: Eerdmans, 1957), 65.
4. Gregory Nazianzen, *Oratio 29* (*LNPF*, 301).

Chapter 4

The Holy Spirit: God's Gift of Love

The Holy Spirit: God's gift of love

When I began seriously to write this book on the mystery of the indwelling Trinity within us, a quaking fear rose up from inside me. The doubt came over me that questioned writing such a book in times such as we are now living in. Would this theme be not reminiscent of the Christian piety of past centuries that so readily could make Christians, eager for deeper prayer, turn inwardly, even into more self-centeredness, without any thrust out into the modern world to become engaged as the light of the world, its very salt? Do we really need another such pious book on God's indwelling presence within our hearts in our modern times of such great international problems that frighten us and yet challenge us to live an active response to the gospel values to bring peace, liberation and justice to all human beings made in God's likeness?

After much prayer and study I came to the conclusion that the revealed doctrine that we and all of creation have come out of the explosive, gracious and free community love of the Holy Trinity is most *practical.* The Trinity is the most basic of all realities. All created realities have come from the foundational reality of the loving triune community. We cannot separate our intellectual assent, given to this most fundamental of all our Christian revealed truths, from our actual living in every thought, word and deed in ever-growing union with the indwelling, immanent Trinity of Father, Son and Spirit.

God separated from his creation

One reason why we Christians make up a very dysfunctional Church has been the vision over centuries of separating our Christian faith from the scientific, material world around us. Our spiritual life was concerned with God's revelation about himself in his inner nature and in his extrinsic relations to us human beings. God revealed the invisible world of heaven that would await us beyond this perishable, material world that all too often was regarded as an obstacle to the spiritual life. Christian virtues gained us graces that would merit for us a high reward in heaven.

Science and religion divided the same world that they both investigated, but with different methods. The material world became separated from its Creator and final goal in the thinking of most scientists and Christians of the past centuries. Spiritual teachers so often failed to preach and teach that the present, material world was also the "place" of the trinitarian action in human history. Creation had a divine purpose and was under divine guidance of his powerful, harmonizing love. Creation would be brought to its completion in becoming the loving community of the body of Christ, the Church, in and through Jesus Christ and the Holy Spirit.

I am convinced that we Christians are urgently in need of discovering the active presence of the triune persons as the source of the material cosmos. We are called by God to love the Creator. But we are to assist in transfiguring matter so as to reflect the immanent Trinity within all of God's material world.

The Trinity relates to the created world

If we truly believe that the same Trinity, Father, Son and Spirit, who dwell within us individuals and in the Church, dwell also in their material world as in a sacred temple, then we must be guided by the threefold presence of the Trinity to the world.

First, from scripture both in the Old and New Testaments we believe that the entire, created universe comes from God and is being sustained by the actively, involved Trinity as creation is being uttered by the Godhead into being by his Word. The Trinity of one divine, loving nature is constantly calling into greater being this universe toward a loving unity by the creative Spirit of God's love.

Second, the universe is destined by the Trinity to be guided toward the Trinity as its goal since the whole cosmos is an immense symbol of the Trinity's revelation to us. Science and religion, when united and not separated from each other, make possible the highest, most transcendent religious experiences of the Trinity. We Christians are especially called through infused faith, hope and love by the Holy Spirit to discover the Trinity's active presence within all of creation. We are invited to work in a *synergism,* a working together, to bring all of God's creation into full completion through the same Jesus Christ and his Holy Spirit.

Third, more specifically, as we discover the immanent Trinity of Father, Son and Spirit within the historical world of the present, we also discern that it has been the same Trinity as working in the historical past up to the present time. We Christians are to live and creatively work according to the Spirit's gifts given each of us to bring about a greater refulgence of the Trinity in and through the universe. Our present world is blanketed by clouds of death, sufferings and moral evils that inflict injustices upon ever mounting numbers of human beings. Such a present world holds us captive in a fearful pessimism that denies the immanent, creative and redeeming power of God in Jesus Christ through the Spirit of love.

The Spirit searches into the depths of God

In this chapter we wish to discover the personhood of the Third Person of the Trinity, the Holy Spirit, in relationship to the Father and Son. We will discover in God's revelation from the images found in scripture and tradition, including the writings of the Fathers of the Church, the saints and theologians and the Church's liturgies what the very first page of the story of Genesis reveals: " . . . and God's spirit hovered over the water" (Gn 1:2).

It is the Spirit who harmonizes chaos into a loving unity. He draws out of darkness light. He gives life to what was dormant or dead. We can discover the immanence of the Trinity, Father, Son and Holy Spirit, working in all of material creation only through the illumination of the Holy Spirit. Paul highlights this revealing power of the Spirit in his words:

These are the very things that God has revealed to us through the Spirit, for the Spirit reaches the depths of everything, even the depths of God. After all, the depths of a man can only be known by his own spirit, not by any other man, and in the same way the depths of God can only be known by the Spirit of God. Now instead of the spirit of the world, we have received the Spirit that comes from God, to teach us to understand the gifts that he has given us. (1 Co 2:10-13)

Who is the Spirit?

Of the three persons of the Trinity, the Holy Spirit seems to us to be the most "impersonal," the one who is most difficult for us to imagine with our mental concepts or to relate to from our own human relationships. All three divine persons are spirits and are invisible to us. Yet we do somehow or other relate to the Son and the Father since such mutual relationships between our earthly father and our own sonship or daughtership relationships are experiential and can give us a human knowledge that presents us with real elements in the nature of the divine Father and the only-begotten Son of the Trinity.

But when we hear the term, Holy Spirit, there is nothing in our human experiences that can suggest anything familiar to us. In scripture and in tradition, the Spirit has not been revealed in a personalized way similar to the way in which the Father and the Son have been revealed to us through the incarnate Word. Thus it is most difficult for us to imagine the Spirit as a real person, known to us by analogous, but experiential knowledge from our own human experience.

Yet we can have absolute certainty about the existence of the Holy Spirit as a person, distinct from the Father and the Son, through the symbols revealed in scripture. The Spirit is discovered in and through the different ways of his acting as revealed through the archetypal symbols of scripture.

Yves Congar, O.P., gives us a list of some of these biblical archetypal symbols that reveal the nature of the Holy Spirit through the activities of the Spirit, analogously found in the symbols used.[1] The Spirit is symbolized as wind, breath, water and fire, as a cloud and a pillar of fire, as the "finger" of God and as the seal and gift of the Father and Son to us.

The value of such symbols to depict the Holy Spirit lies in the fact that they lead us into the mystery of the Spirit with some knowledge without locking us into the objective, scientific language of clear and distinct ideas.

Neglect of the Holy Spirit

No doubt such symbols as the source of our knowledge of the Holy Spirit is the main reason why theology about the Spirit has suffered from much neglect and has always been one of the most difficult doctrines for theologians to present and for the faithful to relate to. Even in the forward-looking Second Vatican Council, we see 158 scattered references to the Holy Spirit. Yet there is not even a complete paragraph, chapter or decree that presents us with a unified and relevant teaching on the Holy Spirit.

Yet today we see the stirrings among those Christians involved in the Charismatic Renewal and among certain Catholic theologians to discover the hidden presence and activities of the Holy Spirit in modern life in terms of the psychological model of personhood.

No doubt the greatest deterrent in presenting the nature of the Holy Spirit, as the transforming love of the Father and the Son who divinizes us into the very community of the Trinity, came through the medieval, scholastic presentation both of the Holy Spirit and the Trinity. The four Aristotelian categories to explain any causality (material, formal, efficient and final causes) were used to explain both the actions of the Trinity outside of itself toward the created world and also to describe the operations of the individual, divine persons indwelling us through created grace. Created grace, as habitual and sanctifying, was objectivized away from the personal love relationships of the trinitarian persons toward us.

Inter-personalism

Today theologians, as Heribert Mühlen, S.J.,[2] Karl Rahner, S.J.,[3] and
a host of others, are returning to the apophatic approach of the early
Eastern Fathers as Basil, Athanasius, Pseudo-Dionysius, Hilary Poitiers, to express the dynamic interpersonal relations that exist within the
Trinity among Father, Son and Holy Spirit and, therefore, of each divine
person, especially of the Holy Spirit, in his relationships with us human
beings in a similar intimate, interpersonal communication and communion.

Using the model proposed in the twelfth century by Richard of St.
Victor (+1173), we can better understand the nature of the Holy Spirit.
We have already seen in the preceding chapter the three characteristics
of intimate love that should predominate in all true, loving friendships,
especially beginning with the primary loving community of all that
consequently shares in that love, namely, availability, mutuality and
self-sacrificing on behalf of the beloved.

If the Father loves the Son and the Son returns the total gift of himself
in self-emptying love to the Father, we have an *I-thou* community. But
such ecstatic, self-emptying love flowing from the Father to the Son and
vice versa cannot be a created love. It must have subsistence and receive
a unique *I-ness* in a vital relationship that proceeds from the Father and
the Son, forming an *I-thou-we* community of three persons equally
loving each other.

Richard of St. Victor explains the necessity of the Spirit as the Third
Person of the Trinity:

> When one gives love to another and when he alone loves the
> other alone, there is love certainly but not shared love. When two
> love each other and give each other their most ardent affection and
> when the affection of the first flows to the second and that of the
> second to the first, moving as it were in different directions, there
> is love on both sides certainly, but there is not shared love. Strictly
> speaking, there is shared love when two persons love a *third* in a
> harmony of affections and a community of love they have for the
> third. . . . From this, then, it is evident that shared love would not

have a place in the divinity if there were only two persons and not a third.[4]

True love must be shared to be real

True love is driven to a transcendence, a pass-over, both from a solitary self-love and a selfish love *a deux* where two persons love each other, but build up barriers and walls to prevent any true sharing of this love outward toward at least one other. By two persons loving each other and sharing that love creatively to call another person into being, we can see that this is not only the law of losing one's life to beget life outside of oneself or two selves experienced in human love relationships in marriage and in friendships, but it must be true, above all, within the family of God.

The Son wishes to love the Father with a perfect, mutual love of total self-sacrifice for him just as the Father loves the Son.[5] It would be an imperfection between the Father and the Son if their love did not want to be shared with another. But to share this mutual love, there is need of a *condilectum,* one that is loved equally as the Father loves the Son and the Son loves the Father. This is the Holy Spirit.[6]

The philosopher, Dietrich von Hildebrand, explains how the *we-relationship* builds upon the *I-thou* as the foundation, making with a third in a "common performance of acts and attitudes."[7] The Father not only knows himself in his Son, but acknowledges himself as uniquely the Son's Father. The opposition between the Father and Son only increases the intimacy the more each person acknowledges both his own uniqueness and also that of the other. Teilhard de Chardin declared that "love differentiates as it unites."[8]

As the uniqueness of each person increases the intimacy and the desire for greater union, love is generated and brings about the union. But, as we have pointed out, this love cannot be a "thing," something created within the Trinity. It must be the personalized *Act* of self-emptying love coming out of the mutual love of the Father and Son, loving each other in the bonding of their mutual Spirit.

Thus it is clear from the nature of the Spirit within the Trinity that the Spirit "proceeds" from the union of the two and brings about the mutual love of the Father and Son. It is this *kenotic* or self-emptying love that constitutes the personalized Third Person of the Trinity, the gift of love from the Father to the Son and the Son to the Father. His being as a person within the Trinity consists in being the act of union and distinction between the Father and Son. In this continued, unchanging "action," the Spirit finds his whole personhood, his unique self, as different from the unique fatherhood and sonship of the other two persons. Thus the Spirit, as Love personified, can never be considered apart from the loving relationship of the Father and Son.

The immanent relationships within the Trinity

We must dwell on the intimate triune relationships between the Father and Son in and through the Spirit's proceeding from both to each other as love in bonding and in self-emptying. We may then understand that these very triune relationships that grant unique personhood in the one community, the Trinity, must be the same relationships of the unique Father and the unique Son and the unique Holy Spirit in the history of salvation, which we will develop more in detail in the subsequent chapters.

Speaking the Word in eternal silence through his out-pouring love that is his Holy Spirit, the heavenly Father hears his Son-Word come back to him in a perfect, eternal yes of total, surrendering love, that is again the Holy Spirit. The theological controversy between the Orthodox and the Catholic Churches about the *filioque* (whether the Holy Spirit proceeds from the Father alone or also from the Son), is no controversy when contemplated in the eternal begetting of God's Son-Word in God's love, the Spirit by the Father-source.

Both Churches hold a partial statement of the truth. The contemplative, who stands before this sacred mystery, knows in a knowledge given only by God's Spirit that the Holy Spirit proceeds as love from the Father and in that same proceeding act of love, the Word-Son is eternally spoken, known and loved. But the Son echoes this divine love as he, the Word-Son, goes back to the Father in and through the same divine Spirit.

The Spirit originates from the Father, but through the mediation of the Son that forms the *I-thou* community and through the Spirit attains a *we*-community.

The Spirit not to be objectivized

Thus, we understand the Holy Spirit, not as a separate person within the Trinity, but in the light of the unity and distinction between the Father and the Son, as the one who brings about through mutual love the *we*-community. We can see that in one sense we should not speak to the Holy Spirit as ourselves speaking to an objective person, separable from the dynamic of inter-personal relationships of the Spirit as bonding love between the Father and the Son toward us. It would be more theologically correct, not to pray *to* the Spirit, but only pray to the Father and the Son to release their Spirit. We pray *in* the Spirit.

The Spirit, therefore, can never be objectivized and spoken to, but he must be experienced in the circular movement of love between the Father and the Son. We can now understand why historically in the great ecumenical councils the dogma about the divinity of the Holy Spirit and his relationship with the Father and Son (and also with us human beings) could only have been articulated after the great christological dogmas about the oneness in essence of the Son with the Father and the hypostatic union of the two natures, divine and human, in the one person of Jesus Christ, had been clarified.

This is no doubt due to the lack of clarity found in scripture to describe the Holy Spirit through his operations in the created world. It also means that a dogma that depends totally upon other dogmas cannot be clarified until such prior doctrines have been clearly enunciated. The implications of the Holy Spirit in his essence in relationship to the Father and the Son within the Trinity and to the order of salvation toward us human beings could have been drawn only when the full divinity of the Son, of the same nature as of the Father, an equal *I-thou* community, was firmly established.

The Holy Spirit as self-emptying love

In conclusion, it is there within the Trinity of an *I-thou-we* community that we must first contemplate the activities of the Holy Spirit as the gift of bonding love between the Father and the Son. For the very gift of God's Spirit to us is the gift that "goes forth" in self-emptying love from the Father to the Son. The true nature of love is not to have a "face," but to be experienced in the *kenotic* or self-emptying between two persons.

No image, no word, no symbol or sign can truly surround the Holy Spirit with seeming mental walls that shout out: "Here we have captured God's Spirit! He is here and not there. He is this and not that." In humility we approach the burning bush, take off our shoes and fall down in adoration to be enlightened by the invisible Spirit of God, who is always operating as loving activity in every facet of God's created world. His works of love are visible and experienced only in our intimate oneness with him as we purify ourselves of our own deluded power to know him as an object. In utter emptiness of heart we wait for the wind, the fire, the living waters to rush upon us and reveal himself in deed as emptying *love* binding the Father and the Son together into a unity of love that brings forth uniqueness, not only of the different Father and the Son but also brings forth his own personhood in such self-emptying. Now we can focus on the full Trinity's relationships to us and the created order of salvific history.

Notes

1. Yves Congar, O.P., *I Believe in the Holy Spirit*, trans. David Smith (New York: The Seabury Press, 1983), 3:4.
2. Cf. H. Mühlen, *Der Heilige Geist als Person* (Münster: Aschendorff, 1966).
3. K. Rahner, *The Trinity* (New York: Herder & Herder, 1969).
4. Richard of St. Victor, *De Trinitate*, bk. 3, chap. 19 (*PL* 196.915B-930D).
5. *Ibid.*, 138.
6. *Ibid.*, 147.
7. Dietrich von Hildebrand, *Metaphysik der Gemeinschaft* (Regensberg: J. Habbell, 1935), 34.
8. Teilhard de Chardin, *The Phenomenon of Man*, trans. Bernard Wall (London: Wm. Collins Sons & Co., 1959), 264-67.

Chapter 5

Uncreated Energies of Divine Love

Uncreated energies of divine love

We are seeing in our various religious groups and in international summit meetings, convened to construct an international peace and justice among all nations and all peoples, a new sense of moving away from our own self-centered "rugged individualism." We are discovering what Dr. John Macmurray, the British philosopher, has pointed out, that the basic unit of personal existence is, not the individual, but two persons in personal relation. We are persons, not by individual right but in virtue of our relation to one another.[1]

Macmurray characterizes the ideal of a community of an *I-thou* or a world community in these personalistic terms:

> It is a universal community of persons in which each cares for all the others and no one for himself. This ideal of the personal is also the condition of freedom—that is, of a full realization of his capacity to act for every person. Short of this there is unintegrated, and therefore suppressed, negative motivation; there is unresolved fear; and fear inhibits action and destroys freedom.[2]

Christianity is a religion that exalts the importance of persons. Indeed our very use of the word "person" of an individual stems from the ancient Christian controversies about the incarnation. The Latin word *persona* from which our word "person" comes, meant "mask" or "legal person," i.e., an entity that could make contracts such as a legally responsible individual or a business corporation. It was in the crucible of theological debates in the early Church about the incarnation that the word *persona* came to mean "person" as we understand it today.

In such debates about the true meaning of Christ and the Trinity we see how the word and concept "person" was used in two ways. In Jesus

43

there is one person and two substances. Why did the early Fathers fight so strenuously against heretical positions about the one person of Jesus Christ and the two natures, divine and human? The right teaching from revelation in scripture and handed down through the traditions taught by the Church hierarchs was that if the death of Jesus was not equally attributable to the whole person, human and divine, then God has not suffered and died for us and we still are unredeemed.

In the doctrine of the Trinity there are three distinct persons, Father, Son and Holy Spirit, but only one substance or divine nature. We see it is always the concept of person that is preeminent in importance over the substance. We are called to share in the divine nature, but of the Father, Son and Holy Spirit as they equally divinize us through grace to become really "children of God" (1 Jn 3:1). It is only the Second Person of the Trinity, the only-begotten Son of the Father, who became in that eternal person human, one person in two distinct but inseparable natures. This whole person has died and has been raised up by the Father in transfiguring glory and now lives in his Church, in the sacraments, and in each Christian, one in substance with the Father and the Spirit who, therefore, also dwell within us.

Why does God create?

Only because of the three persons making up the Trinity can we ever understand why God creates this material world and entrusts it to us human beings to cooperate with God's eternal purpose. When the question is asked of God's free decision to create a material world outside of the perfect, holy, all-beautiful community of trinitarian love, the answer can only be rooted in the fact that God is love. God is a circle that knows no circumference.

Within that infinite, perfect circle of loving persons, as we have established in the preceding chapters, each divine person lives for the others. Each finds uniqueness only in giving oneself away in *kenotic* or self-emptying love for the others. To be both gift and giver, individual persons must be free from all outside coercion or force. The gift of self in true love must be completely gratuitous.

These two words, *love* and *freedom*, touch on the basic, awesome mystery of the Trinity, both within the intrinsic, trinitarian relationships and in extrinsic relationships toward us, God's chosen children. True love and true freedom can never be separated. To love freely is the way God is God. God's being consists in his nature as the one-who-loves in freedom. God exercises his freedom in his-being-love. But since the essence of God is to be one, loving nature in three persons, the Father, Son and Holy Spirit have their existence in freely exercising their self-emptying love for each other.

God's perfect love toward us

Tied to the mysterious makeup of God as an *I* that is also a *we*, is God's free choice to wish to share his divine nature, his holiness and beauty by creating creatures outside of himself in order to share, especially with his angelic and human creatures, his very own inner, trinitarian life and happiness. The perfect, implosive love within the Trinity freely wishes to explode out in creation in order to become "othered" in limited creatures, who can manifest the divine perfections and on various levels can participate in those perfections.

God spills out his trinitarian love in activity in the creation of human beings and the universe, in the incarnation of his divine Son, Jesus Christ, in the redemption by the God-man of the whole human and subhuman cosmos, in the sanctification and final *parousia* through the Holy Spirit. These are all free actions of God prompted by the one constant act of love.

Chosen for his glory

God has freely chosen us that we might share in his glory. When God raised Jesus from the dead and "raised him high and gave him the name which is above all other names" (Ph 2:9), his humanity was brought into a perfect oneness with his divinity and a new oneness with the triune life.

We, too, by God's goodness have been made to share in the very life of the triune family. God has not created us merely to be "good" people, who do good things in order to attain heaven. He has created us to share in his ecstatic happiness. His love permeates, invades, bombards us at all times as the three divine persons "go out of themselves" in order that we might "be able to share the divine nature" (2 P 1:4). As human beings, created freely by God according to his own image and likeness (Gn 1:26-22), we stand erect among all other creatures, capable of knowing God's personalized love for each of us individually and by grace to return that love. We are called by God to contemplate God's loving, gifting presence of himself to us in intimate communion and to find our uniqueness and ecstatic happiness by becoming a loving, gifted presence to all those around us.

Before we can do good things and become holy people as God is good and holy, we must experience through God's Spirit of love how greatly at every moment we are being loved infinitely by God's triune community. A tree cannot be urged by the fruit grower to bring forth good fruit unless the tree from roots to branches is a totally good tree in its being. Then good fruit will naturally come from that state of being a good tree. So we must grow in ever increasing awareness through the Spirit of the Trinity's personalized love for us individually and then wish freely to share that unique, beautiful person in a similar "going forth" to share the gift of ourselves with God and neighbor.

All emptying love

God's pursuing love for us, his readiness to forget and empty himself completely in order to fill us with himself as gift, is seen in his suffering love, revealed and manifested to us in human terms in Jesus crucified. Nowhere has God's revealed love reached a greater peak of fiery heat and self-giving to us than in the image of Jesus on the cross, totally broken, rejected and poured out for love of us.

Before such humble, *kenotic* love, we can only whisper in shuddering faith, as Paul did, that he "loved me and sacrificed himself for my sake" (Ga 2:20).

Part of the ecstasy of God's love for us is not only his moving toward us in complete self-giving, but in his vulnerability as he patiently waits for our response. "Love is always patient and kind . . . it is always ready to excuse, to trust, to hope, and to endure whatever comes" (1 Co 13:4-7). To love is to be humble. Love can never be completed only in the giving. For God to love us is freely to wish us to share his happiness. But in order that we can share divine life, we must be free humbly to return God's love. Thus God, who by his nature is totally independent and complete in his perfect being, humbly makes himself vulnerable as he truly waits to be loved by us. It is not that he is deficient and we, by loving him, can offer him his completion. But in awesome humility God freely loves us and ties our happiness to his freely chosen need to receive our love in return.

Jesus said, "The Father himself loves you" (Jn 16:27). God's love is availability to give love, but he makes himself humbly available to receive in need our returned love. We have the power to complete God's ecstasy by calling him into the state of being loved by us as we live in oneness with his only-begotten Son and through their mutual Spirit can become truly children of God, heirs of heaven and co-heirs with Christ forever (Rm 8:15).

All this is a mystery and the work of the hidden, emptying Spirit of love, who "reaches the depths of everything, even the depths of God" (1 Co 2:11). This is the "hidden wisdom of God" (1 Co 2:7) that Paul preached as wisdom of the spiritually matured. Such is a darkness of our own intellectual abilities and a light by faith to believe that God is not only ecstatically in love with each of us in his constant self-giving, but he humbly waits for our return of love.

When we realize by the Spirit that God really wants our love and needs us in a sense to bring him into his being *our* Father, our lives change. God's Spirit of love gives us an inner transformation of mind and heart to experience what Jesus in his human life experienced. We, too, as Jesus did and with the risen Jesus living within us in his Spirit, can live according to the dignity to which God has called us, to live in ecstatic happiness as we go out of our selfishness to accept God's gift of himself, but also as we seek "to act justly, to love tenderly and to walk humbly with your God" (Mi 6:8).

How does God relate to us?

The perennial question theology always poses is: How does God, who is perfect, immutable, inaccessible to his creatures in his invisible and incomprehensible essence, meet us, his creatures, and share with us his nature? How does God work in the created order, he who is infinite, eternal, transcendent and beyond all time and space? If God is completely transcendent, how can he be inside of us and his creation, limiting himself to our finiteness?

One way of answering this question is that put forth by most Western Christian theologians who have followed the scholastic theology inherited from the Middle Ages of Thomas Aquinas. Thomas viewed God's relations with the material, created world, including us human beings, as based on Aristotle's static concepts of nature, substance and matter. Thomas writes: "God's temporal relations to creatures are in him only because of our way of thinking of him; but the opposite relations of creatures to him are realities in creatures."[3]

The weakness of such a theological view lies in its inability to bring God, as scripture does, into a personalized relationship in temporality and in matter with us. Such a perspective ignores the biblical view of God as a loving Father who truly relates intimately and is completely involved with every facet of our lives. He is a God toward us as also is his image, Jesus Christ, a man toward others.

God's uncreated energies

Let us look at the important perspective of the early Eastern Fathers that is rooted in scripture that is at the basis of any and all of God's inter-personal relationships with us human beings and all of his creation. This is the distinction of the Eastern Fathers between God's *essence* and his *uncreated energies*.[4]

Some Eastern Fathers carefully distinguish between the essence of God that is one nature, equally shared by the three divine persons, and God's own nature as the ground of being in the multiplied world of creation. Pseudo-Dionysius described the movement outwardly toward the created world as a "going forth" of God (*proodos* in Greek). The importance of this distinction is rooted in God's revelation. His essence no human being can see or comprehend in any human fashion. No human being has ever seen God and lived (Ex 33:23; 1 Jn 4:12; Jn 1:18; 6:46). Yet the good news of God's revelation is that he lovingly wishes to share his very own being with us. This he does through his divine, uncreated energies of love. These uncreated energies are not something which exists outside of God. They are not even some extrinsic gift God gives us. They are God himself in his action, God in his active revelation as gift of love to his creatures.

The divine energies are uncreated as is the essence of God. The essence of God is the cause or reason of the energies. This distinction between the essence and the energies in God does not compromise anything of the unity of God, of his integrity and simplicity. The essence and energies are not "two parts" of God, but they are two ways, two means of God's existence. The divine energies belong to the three divine persons. They are common to them as is the divine essence common to the three persons of the Trinity. Uncreated energies are also called "powers" or "manifestations" of God.[5]

God in self-giving

God's energies, therefore, are really God in his loving relationships toward us. In God his activities can never be divided as we divide activities into those that are sacred and those that are merely secular, between those that are natural and those that are supernatural. The energies are God, who in his essence is unapproachable and simple, yet who in his condescending love is always (hence uncreated) manifesting himself to us in diverse ways. They are God's way of showing himself in self-giving to us human beings.

Archbishop Joseph Raya of the Melchite Byzantine Rite, gives us a beautiful description of God's energies that summarizes well the Eastern patristic teaching:

It is not God's action but God himself in his action who makes
himself known to man and gives him the ability to "see" him. God
enters into man's love, remaining there in his intimate reality. This
presence is real, indeed most real. This communication of God
himself is called "Uncreated Energy." The uncreated energies of
God are not "things" which exist outside of God, not "gifts" of
God; they are God himself in his action. They are the very God
who is himself Uncreated. They are therefore called "uncreated"
because their cause and origin is the Essence of God. In them God
as it were goes beyond himself and becomes "transradiant" in
order really to communicate himself. Thus the Essence and energies of God are not "parts" of God but two ways by which we
human beings can contemplate God's essence.[6]

The economy of salvation

We can see, therefore, how important is the distinction between
God's essence as totally beyond our knowledge and comprehension and
God's uncreated energies of love which are the means of the unique
persons of the Trinity in one united nature of perfect love, touching us
as the divine persons relate to us in self-giving love. Thus we can truly
experience the trinitarian persons, know them through the grace of the
uncreated energies and become divinized or deified, as we shall point
out in the next chapter.

God not only deemed to reveal the truth of the mystery of the Trinity
to us, but in that revelation he has made the mystery of the Trinity the
beginning and the end of all reality. God effects our fulfillment to
divinize us precisely in and through the activities of the triune God in
the context of our history of salvation.

We come, not only to know, but also to experience the triune God
within what Karl Rahner calls the biblical data about the "economic"
Trinity. The word *economia* (*oikonomia* in Greek) etymologically refers
to any divine activity in relationship to creatures. Thus theologians
speak of "the economy of salvationship." Among the Eastern Fathers,
theology properly so-called concerns itself with teaching about the
Divine Being itself, the Holy Trinity, within itself as revealed by Jesus

Christ, and outside in its vital self-giving to us. The exterior manifestations of God, the Holy Trinity, known in its relation to created beings, belong to the realm of economy.[7]

Rahner recalls to us the principle that was taken for granted by Eastern Christian theologians: "The 'economic Trinity' is the 'immanent Trinity' and the 'immanent Trinity' is the 'economic' Trinity."[8] In identifying the Trinity of the economy of salvation with the immanent Trinity (the life within the very Trinity of the Father, Son and Holy Spirit, without any reference to the created order), Rahner, along with the early Eastern Fathers and M. Scheeben, seeks to stress the personalism of the three divine persons in their one "essential" act of self-communication to us human beings.

If this were not true, Rahner argues, "God would be the 'giver,' not the gift itself, he would 'give himself' only to the extent that he communicates a gift distinct from himself."[9]

Thus we can affirm and believe that God as Trinity in his essence is the giver while God in his intimate relationships to us gives himself as gift in his energies by which God can be known outside himself in his self-giving relationships to us. These energies are inseparable from the divine essence which the energies manifest. God in his uncreated energies is the true gift of grace, uncreated grace.[10]

We can be healed of our fears and forgiven our sins and transformed into real children of God, "Gods by grace,"[11] only if God gives us himself in and through Jesus Christ and the Holy Spirit by means of the triune uncreated energies of love. What hinges very strongly and importantly upon this thesis of the similarity between the immanent, trinitarian "activities (*intra se*)" and the economic "activities" is the question whether we human beings are so loved by God that we are radically transformed by God's gift of himself and by his very own transforming persons, the Son and the Holy Spirit, or whether we are merely extrinsically "affiliated" with God in a salvation of decree and not of true "regeneration." It also avoids our assimilation into an absolute being and thus loving our unique personhood now and in the life to come. God is always God and we are always his human creatures.

Energies of love

The doctrine of the Eastern Fathers concerning grace, primarily as being God, giving himself to us as uncreated energies of love, has much to teach us. If we are to live in the mystery of God's love in each moment, then we must find him essentially as one God, loving us with an everlasting, unchanging love. But if this love is to transform us into loving persons, who can live in the mystery of oneness and uniqueness toward all human beings that we meet, then these loving energies must also bring us into the personal and unique love activities of the three persons.

God's love will too easily be objectivized as a thing with which he loves us unless the Father is now experienced by us as begetting us into new life in his only-begotten Son, through their mutual Spirit of love. How can we experience God's triune activities of one nature, as loving gift to us in and through the uncreated energies of God, but also how can we experience the unique and personal gift of the Father, different from the Son's personal gift of himself as the only-begotten Son, and both different from the Holy Spirit, who gives himself as self-emptying love of one Father and Son in us? We must understand finally the importance of the mystery of the incarnation of the Son of God and man who is the only bridge between the Trinity and ourselves.

Appropriations

We must begin by understanding the term *appropriations*, used by theologians since the time of Augustine. This refers to our assigning a certain power or quality to one of the three divine persons, even though as we have said, any action of God is of God's essential energy of love and is common to all three persons. However, because of a similarity between that given quality and the distinct, personalized relationship within the Trinity certain attributes are assigned by theologians and spiritual writers to individual persons.

Thus power is associated with the Father since he is the source of the processions of the Son and Holy Spirit. Wisdom is assigned to the Son since he proceeds as the Word and image of the Father. Goodness is associated with the Holy Spirit since he is the fullness and loving completion of the Trinity and God's gift to us in whom all gifts are given.[12]

What is important to remember in linking appropriations with the uncreated energies is that such attributes flow from the total, divine essence and are not "personalized" qualities predicated solely to any one of the persons of the Trinity. To understand what is personal and proper to each member of the Trinity, as Bonaventure wrote, Christian faith is required.[13]

In terms of Eastern Christian theology all actions that flow from the divine energies are common to all three divine persons. From our viewpoint, the manifestations of these energies are multiple. From that of the Trinity, there is one, divine energy attributable to the divine essence, therefore, to the common action of all three persons. Gregory Palamas uses the example of the one sun giving off a ray that equally gives warmth, light, life and nourishment.[14]

The mystery of the incarnation

The greatest revelation of the three persons' relationships to all of creation, especially to us human beings, took place in the mystery of the incarnation. God so loved this world as to give us his only-begotten Son, so that whoever believed in him would have eternal life (Jn 3:16). He is through his humanity the image of what the Word images always from all eternity from within the Trinity.

We must not view God's actions in time and historical space when he decreed the incarnation so that it may seem as an afterthought, decided on by the Trinity in order to remedy the sinful situation caused by the fall or our first parents. Rather, we must believe in the words of Paul: "Before the world was made, he chose us, chose us in Christ, to be holy and spotless, and to live through love in his presence, determining that we should become his adopted sons through Jesus Christ" (Eph 1:4-5).

The incarnation gives us the fullness of God's revelation through the only-begotten Son, taking on our humanity, one divine person in two distinct, but inseparable natures of divinity and humanity. Without the incarnation we would always have believed that God would touch us and communicate himself to us only through the energies. We would always have been unable to enter into "personalized" relationships with the Father, different from those of the Son and the Holy Spirit, if it had not been for the incarnation. For this mystery reveals to us through the materiality of the human nature of Christ what our own humanity can attain by grace.

This dogma of the hypostatic union teaches us that the Second Person of the Trinity, who operates equally and conjointly with the other two persons in all "energetic" actions throughout the universe, acted on the historical, horizontal level in a unique manner that reflected somewhat his very own oppositional relationships to the Father and the Holy Spirit within the immanent life of the Trinity.

The person of the Word of God, different from the Father and the Spirit, but not separated within the Trinity, assumed a human nature. This nature did not exist of itself and then was merely added somehow to the divine Son of God. In that very act of incarnation the eternal Word gave existence to his human nature and divinized it. This humanity of Jesus Christ had the immortal and incorruptible character of the nature of Adam before he sinned, yet Jesus in that humanity was subjected to the conditions of our fallen natures, as Maximus the Confessor wrote.[15]

Christ is the *Pontifex Maximus,* the greatest of all bridge-builders, who spans the infinite world of God (including the personalized world of the three persons within the Trinity) and the finite world of mankind and created beings. "For the unlimited is limited in an ineffable manner, while the limited is stretched to the measure of the unlimited," wrote Maximus.[16]

Through the revelation of the God-man, Jesus Christ, we can believe that the Second Person as *Logos* has been revealing the hidden Godhead from the beginning of creation with a personalized act different from the Father. The Father and source of all being creates all the created world in and through his Word by the overshadowing of his Spirit of love. "Through him all things came to be, not one thing had its being but through him. All that came to be had life in him" (Jn 1:1-2). The

Word, within the one, energetic manifestation of God, exerts his own proper, personalistic action. Scripture reveals this to us as a specific act of imaging the Father through knowledge discovered throughout all nature and within the intellectual powers of us human beings.

The Word made flesh reflects the eternal Word

But through the incarnation the Second Person continues now through the humanity assumed by the Logos to reveal himself to us through specific actions reflecting that immanent action of the Son within the Trinity.

The human nature of Christ is totally penetrated by the one, divine nature, yet it always remains distinct from that divine nature. It is "existentially" united to the Second Person of the Trinity and not to the first, the Father, nor the third, the Holy Spirit.

Through the incarnation something totally new has happened and still continues to happen for the rest of eternity. Within the very Trinity now humanity is one with the Second Person of the Trinity. The uncreated Word and only-begotten Son of the Father loves him, not only with the fullness of the Son's divine personhood, but he also loves him with the fullness of his human nature in the one person, Jesus Christ. And the Second Person of the Trinity loves us with the fullness of a human consciousness, but also as the same person, God-Son, from all eternity.

God needs the Son incarnate

We have already seen that within the Trinity the Father is not self-existent and independent of the Son and the Spirit. The *I-ness* of the Father is in vital relationship to the Son, both in giving the Love, the Holy Spirit, to the Son, and in waiting for and receiving the free gift of the Son back to the Father in the same Spirit. The three persons within the Trinity are each unique, free and loving persons, who find their personhood, not only by giving oneself as gift to the other, but also in receiving the gift of the other in the return through the bonding Spirit of love.

In order that we can understand that the very immanent relationships within the Trinity as giver and receiver are the same toward us and that we can impact the lives of the trinitarian persons as we not only receive their gifts of their unique, loving persons of the Trinity, but we also offer ourselves as gift from a free, loving person to the trinitarian persons of Father, Son and Holy Spirit, we need to see the different ways the Father needs the gift of the Son of God incarnate.

Through the incarnation in our human time and space, the eternal Father was pleased, not only with his eternal Son, but also by the total person, the God-man, who, as completely divine and human, thrilled the heart of the Father. The Father waited on the free choices of his Son to be "othered," not only as the Father of this eternal Son, but also as the Father of this Son incarnate. His beloved Son, both in his divinity and humanity, one person, in time and space, within the human race, does whatever pleases the Father.

The Father is pleased because in his infinite wisdom he himself would have chosen such acts of complete self-emptying even unto the last drop of blood, if he had a body. It is the Father who is imaged to each of us in the torn, mangled body of Jesus, hanging on the cross and crying out in the agony of seeming abandonment by the Father who loved him so much: "See, I have branded you on the palms of my hands" (Is 49:16).

When Jesus was freely baptized by John in the river Jordan, one with the sinful race of human persons, the Father's voice rang out: "This is my Son, the beloved, with whom I am well pleased" (Mt 3:17).

Transfigured in glory on Mount Tabor, Jesus, after he had foretold to his disciples his imminent suffering, death and resurrection, was covered with a luminous cloud, and the three disciples heard the Father speak: "This is my beloved Son, with whom I am well pleased" (Mt 17:5).

God needs you

The incarnate Word made flesh, Jesus Christ, in his divine and human natures, but as one whole person, identical as the divine Second Person of the Trinity, returns himself to the eternal Father. Yet now through his humanity he can add a new dimension of joy and completion to the

Father as *this* Father of *this* divine-human Son through his Spirit. Now perhaps we can understand how we can say that we can also in some way impact the life of God.

Once Jesus has died and has risen from the dead, exalted by the Father, he can now pour out his Spirit upon us so we can understand in him the infinite, perfect love of the Father for us. In his Spirit we know we belong to Christ. We form one body with him (Eph 4:4-6; Jn 15:5), and in his Spirit and our oneness with Jesus, we can bear fruit that pleases the Father.

When we love others in the self-sacrificing love of Jesus in his Spirit, it is not only we ourselves, but it is we, members of his very own body, the Church, in and with and for Christ that we are able to thrill the heavenly Father. We are filling up the total Christ, he the head, but we his members. The Father is waiting and eagerly longs for the total Christ to come back to him in an emptying love that will thrill for all eternity the Father and transform him into the unique Father of the unique total Jesus Christ, you and me in Christ, pleasing the Father for all eternity, but even now in our time and space impacting the Father, Son and Spirit, as we respond to the Trinity's uncreated energies of love.

Now we are able to advance to the most important subject of the Trinity's work, in and through the divine energies of love in the context of our daily life, to deify or divinize us (*theosis* in Greek) into participators of God's very own nature (2 P 1:4). Athanasius, quoting Irenaeus' statement, summarizes the answer to the "why" of the incarnation, but also the purpose of why God has created us:

> The Divine Word was made man that we might become gods. He was made visible through his body in order that we might have an idea of the invisible Father. He has supported the outrages of men in order that we may have a part of his immortality.[17]

Notes

1. Dr. John Macmurray, *Persons in Relation,* The Gifford Lectures of 1953-54, (London: Faber & Faber and New York: Harpers, 1961), 1:61.
2. *Ibid.,* 159.
3. Thomas Aquinas, *Summa Theologiae,* Prima Pars, 13, 7 ad 4.
4. There is an ever increasing literature on this subject of God's uncreated energies, found predominantly among Eastern Christian theologians, but practically unknown to Western Christians. See my work, *A Theology of Uncreated Energies* (Milwaukee, WI: Marquette University, 1978).
5. Cf. M. Lot-Borodine, "La doctrine de la deification dans l'Eglise greque jusqu'au Xie siécle," in: *La deification de l'homme* (Paris, 1970, end edition), 30 ff.
6. Archbishop Joseph Raya, *The Face of God* (Denville: Dimension Books, 1976), 37-8.
7. Cf. V. Lossky, *The Mystical Theology of the Eastern Church* (Cambridge & London: James Clarke & Co., 1957), 71.
8. K. Rahner, *The Trinity,* 22.
9 *Ibid.,* 101.
10. Cf. Roland Zimany, "Grace, Deification and Sanctification: East-West," in *Diakonia* (1977), 12:125.
11. Symeon the New Theologican (+1022) Catecheses, in Basile Krivocheine ed. and trans., *Sources Chrétiennes Series* (Paris: Cerf, 1963) 96:40.
12. Augustine, *De Trinitate* 5.8-9.
13. Bonaventure, *Quaestiones Disputatae de Mysterio Trinitatis* 1 sent., d. 3, p. 1, a. un., q. 4.
14. Gregory Palamas, *Capita Physica* 68 (*PG* 150.1169).
15. Maximus the Confessor, *Quaestiones ad Thalassium* 21 (*PG* 90.312-316).
16. Maximus the Confessor, *Epistola* XXI (*PG* 91.604 BC).
17. Athanasius, *De Incarnatione Verb* (*PG* 25. 92B).

Chapter 6

The Process of Divinization

The process of divinization

Basically there are two fundamentally different approaches to the Holy Trinity and its relationships to us human beings. Our Western approach is predominantly to begin with the nature of God as perfect, immutable, pure Spirit. In the history of salvation by the sin of our proto-parents, we lost all supernatural and preternatural virtues. Now God must reconstruct the supernatural order for us by giving us created, sanctifying and actual graces that will extrinsically make us worthy to respond and to receive redemption.

The Eastern Christian approach, using the scriptural model of imageness and likeness, starts with God, through the revelation made by the incarnate Word, Jesus Christ, as a community of three unique persons in a unity of one nature. This community wishes to share the unique personhood of each in a similar unity of love with us human beings.

Sin did not destroy the goal God has always had for us human beings. It has weakened our ability to respond to God's uncreated energies of love. The *imago Dei* (the imageness of God) can never be lost in any of us, since it is the most inward nature of what it truly means for us to be human. It is, in the terminology of Karl Rahner, the "existential supernatural" that is indestructible. This imageness, as a potential to mature and grow into a greater likeness of God-Trinity, is God's gifting presence within us.

The *likeness* is not yet accomplished, for this actuation of the imageness into a conscious, inter-personal relationship between the Father, Son and Holy Spirit and the individual human person cannot be realized unless we cooperate with the divinizing grace of the Holy Spirit. The Spirit creates the inner, deepest-down "place" where, by the Spirit's faith, hope and love and our own striving freely to respond to God's uncreated energies, we can consciously live in loving union with the indwelling Trinity.

A cat and rat story

As I was pondering these two different approaches of Western and Eastern Christian frameworks, I recalled a story from the annals of Japanese Zen Buddhism. There once was a master swordsman named Shoken. He was plagued by an enormous rat. He put his cat in the room to do battle and rid him of this pesky rat, but the rat sprang at the cat and bit it in the face and sent it off howling! Shoken then brought in a number of neighborhood cats with good reputations as rat-killers, but all ran away as the rat viciously attacked and bit them.

Shoken then tried to kill the rat by his own power as a swordsman, but the rat dodged him and finally bit him in the face. He sent a messenger to fetch the best rat-killer cat there was in the kingdom. The cat that was presented to Shoken as the very best rat-killer cat in the kingdom looked ever so ordinary that Shoken had no hope of anything special from her. As he cautiously let the cat in, she walked very calmly and slowly into the room as if expecting nothing out of the ordinary.

The big rat gave start, but did not stir. The cat simply walked unhurriedly up to it, picked it up in her mouth, and carried it out. That evening all the defeated cats met in Shoken's house and congratulated the victorious cat. They were curious at her success and asked: "How did you manage to beat it so easily? Please tell us your secret." Before she would answer, she asked them how they had tried to overcome the rat. One cat used all the acrobatic tricks he knew but failed. A large tabby cat used her mental powers to attack the rat, but she too was humiliated in her defeat.

An old gray cat used the power of the heart to make peace with his opponent, by using it as a trick to overcome the rat. But the victorious cat told them they were not wrong in using techniques, but even those had to be surrendered to what was already within as one's true nature.

In conclusion she replied: "And so there is no 'mystery' that a master can pass on to his student. To instruct is easy. To listen is easy. But it is hard to become aware of what one has within oneself, to track it down and take possession of it properly. This is what we call looking into our true nature. When we do this, we experience the great awakening from the dream of error and illusion. To wake, to look into one's nature, to perceive the truth of oneself, all of these are the same thing."

Discovering your true self

Each day of your life is an excellent time to discover your true nature as a divine child of the Trinity that dwells within you. "Children, you have already overcome these false prophets because you are from God and you have in you one who is greater than anyone in this world. But we are children of God" (1 Jn 4:4, 6). We really, even now, are transformed through God the Father coming to us through his two "hands," Jesus Christ and the Holy Spirit, as Irenaeus of the second century described it. This is what the Eastern Fathers called the ongoing process that extends itself even into the life to come, the process of *divinization* or *deification* by grace into participators of God's very own nature (2 P 1:4).

Gods by grace

Basil wished to summarize God's great love in creating us human beings according to his own image and likeness as a summary of what is found in scripture, especially in the New Testament, when he wrote: "Man is the creature who received the order to become God by grace."[1]

Whatever the early Fathers taught about the divinization process, they believed they were grounding their doctrine in scripture. The most often cited passage is John 10:34-34: "Is it not written in your Law: I said, 'You are gods'? So the Law uses the word 'gods' of those to whom the Word of God was addressed." What we should notice is that even in the Old Testament, the guardian of monotheism, the word "gods" (from Ps 82:6), which Jesus here quotes, was applied to all human beings.

Another important text is from 1 John 3:1-2: "We are already the children of God, but what we are to be in the future has not yet been

revealed; all we know is that when it is revealed we shall be like him."
And from 1 John 4:17: ". . . even in this world we have become as he
is."

The quote from 2 Peter 1:4 is the one most developed by the early
Church theologians: ". . . you will be able to share the divine nature."
These words are explained in the texts as entrance into the very divine
life of the Holy Trinity as the process of *divinization*.[2]

Patristic tradition

In the teaching of the early Fathers, who wrote chiefly in Greek, the
most important passage is the sentence of Irenaeus, that would be
developed by the other Orthodox teachers of Eastern theology. "God
became man in order that man might become God."[3] We can find a
similar expression in Athanasius: "The Logos in the Spirit gives to
human beings glory and by deification and adoption leads them to the
Father."[4]

Clement of Alexandria expresses the divinizing goal of the incarnation: "Logos, the Word of God, became man in order that you can learn
through the intercession of Man, how man can become God by grace."[5]
It was Clement of Alexandria, who coined the words *theopoiesis* and
theosis (the process of God, divinizing human beings through grace to
make them divine by participating in God's nature). These words would
be used by all the Greek Fathers. The most adequate explanation of
divinization through the work of the Holy Spirit is found in the writings
of Basil, Pseudo-Macarius and Maximus.[6] Maximus the Confessor
wrote that human beings by divinization have all that God has by nature,
but without the identification of nature.[7]

Participation in divine life

We must keep ever in mind, as we pointed out in the preceding
chapter, that divinization is participation in the divine nature (2 P 1:4),
but this cannot be participation in God's total divine essence. If we could
unite with God's essence we would no longer be human creatures and

God would not be a Trinity of persons. God would have as many persons as those participating in God's essence. Let us be very clear that our human unity with God in divinization is never *pantheism*. Thus we see again the importance of the Eastern Fathers' distinction between God's nature or essence and his divine energies of active love in interpersonal relationships with us.

Divinization of us human beings as sharers in God's very own divine life through grace is made possible in its fullness only in and through the power of the mystery of his incarnation, resurrection and the sending of his Holy Spirit in Pentecost. It is the result of the hypostatic union of the divine and human natures of Jesus Christ in the one personhood of the eternal Son of God.

Our alienation from the divine trinitarian family through sin is done away with and our true filiation with the heavenly Father is restored by Jesus Christ and his Spirit. Now we are offered the great grace of becoming holy and divinized, not by anything intrinsic to our created, human nature as separated from God's energies, but only by our participation with God's grace. Divinization is the free-willed gift of God. Yet it requires our free and conscious cooperation with the Trinity.

This work of our participation in God's divine life is the work of both Christ and the Holy Spirit. The role of sanctifying us is the work of the Holy Spirit in the process of divinization (*theosis*). Yet the Holy Spirit can never be separated from the work of the Father's Son, the Word made flesh, Jesus Christ.

The divinizing work of the Holy Spirit

The work of the Holy Spirit begins and grows as we develop interiorly a docility to surrender to his indwelling guidance, one with that of the Son and the Father. The Holy Spirit becomes more internal for us than we are internally present to ourselves, in the words of the Orthodox theologian, O. Clement.[8] Through the Holy Spirit the will of God does not remain something external to us, but now is manifested by the indwelling Spirit as a guiding voice that reveals to us how our human will is to cooperate with the divine will. This is the essence of divinizaton.

In this work of *theosis,* we see the *kenosis* or self-emptying love of the Spirit revealed to us. The Spirit finds his uniqueness within the Trinity as having no "personalized" relationship to the Father and the Son other than that of proceeding or issuing forth in self-emptying love from them to us human beings. The Holy Spirit is the gift of bonding love between the Father and the Son. The true nature of love is not to have a "face," but to be experienced in the *kenotic* or self-emptying between two persons. The work of the Spirit of love is invisible and experienced only in our intimate oneness with him as we purify ourselves of our own deluded power to know him as an object. In utter emptiness of heart we wait for the wind, the fire, the living waters of the Spirit to rush upon us and reveal himself in deed.

The Holy Spirit enables us Christians to assert as an experienced reality the truth of our divinization, in spite of the contradictory experience of our own nothingness and inner darkness and of God's humble omnipotence. Symeon the New Theologian (+1024) of all the early Greek Fathers stressed in the boldest language the divinizing process whereby we human beings by our cooperation and the grace of God are able to advance continually toward a greater "oneness" with the Trinity dwelling within us.

Boldly Symeon repeats over and over that God's aim in creating us is to make us through the Holy Spirit and Jesus Christ "a god by adoption and grace."

> O strange thing! to be simply men, but what we have become by divine grace is not seen by the multitude.
> It is only to those whose eye of the soul has been purified that we appear such as we are. . . .[9]

Every Christian, guided internally by the Holy Spirit, becomes able to enter into an intimate spousal relationship with Christ, through the community of the Church and the divinizing power of the Paraclete without any absorption or disappearance of our own unique personhood. The perfect gift of the Love, the Spirit, seemingly disappears as he conceals himself in order that we may reach perfect unity in love with Christ and through Christ with the Father. In Christ by the Holy Spirit we become receptacles of the trinitarian act of God as love. Love is the trinitarian persons giving themselves to us in diverse manners of loving. Therefore the way to unity with God is love and divinization through Jesus Christ in the Spirit to the Father. *Theosis* or divinization is the work of the total nature of God as love, sharing through the divine uncreated energies of love, manifested to us human beings, their gift to us of participating in their very divine nature.

Our need to cooperate

An ancient patristic saying is: "God associates only with gods." In order that we can become gods by participation through God's gratuitous grace released by the indwelling Trinity (Jn 14:26), we must cooperate to fulfill certain conditions. We are to be reborn by water and the Holy Spirit (Jn 3:3, 5) and develop into the likeness of Jesus Christ by our continued cooperation in love with God. Although the fullness of the Trinity resides within us through baptism, nevertheless, our awareness in consciousness is brought about by the Spirit's gifts, especially faith, hope and love with our own vigilant cooperation. Thus we can see that there are different degrees of divinization depending upon our cooperation.

As long as we strive, in spite of our weaknesses, to accomplish God's holy will as manifested in fulfilling his commands, we can believe from the First Letter of John 4:17: "Because even in this world we have become as he is." Grace never forces us to act in this or that fixed manner. Grace "allures" us by the attraction of a delicate, yet strong presence through faith, calling us from the depths of our being to come home to our loving Father. The good news is that God is grace, uncreated love, always present within us and around us and acting in a self-emptying gifting of himself to us through the indwelling Spirit.

Grace: a dialogue of loving cooperation

The continued invitations to us from this Spirit are created graces that call us to freely respond. This is the created relationship that, when, in our infirmities, brokenness, fears, doubts, and even sinfulness, we freely will to answer to in faith, trust and love, we can call "sanctifying grace." We freely cooperate, yet even our response is covered with God's enticing love, the Holy Spirit.

We cooperate with the Spirit's graces through the Church, the "place" of divinization. Eastern Christianity, from earliest times, has seen in the divine liturgy and the sacraments, not only the healing for our sinful disintegration, but above all the epiphany and outpouring of divinizing energies.[10]

The theology of the Holy Spirit in his role of divinizer of us human beings is reflected in the liturgical prayer of the Church in the so-called *epiklesis* or the calling down of the Spirit to effect the process of divinization in and through the sacraments. The place of the *epiklesis* is at the heart of every communion with God because, according to the tradition of the Church, we do not have access to the Father except only in the Son and we have access to the Son only by the Holy Spirit.[11] Thus *epiklesis* is necessary.

Not only the sacraments of initiation, baptism, confirmation and eucharist, but every sacrament as well as the entire liturgy of the Church have their divinizing actions.

The way to divinization: praxis

Thus we see that divinization in Christ, with the help of the energies of the Holy Spirit given in the Church, is given in the Church and especially through the sacraments. But the sacraments do not automatically produce their effects in a magical way. Our cooperation is necessary as we strive totally toward the realization of the divine plan to make us participators of the trinitarian, eternal life.

This is called in Christian spirituality *praxis* or *ascesis*.[12] *Praxis* focuses chiefly on two levels of relationships: what we human beings must do to control and purify the negative effects of sin and disintegration through self-love; and secondly through the Spirit to develop the virtues Jesus lived in the gospels as we put on the mind of Christ (Eph 4:17).

Need for inner purification

Jesus insisted that, if we would wish to have a part with him, we would have to deny our false self by taking up our cross and following him. We would have to guard our "heart," the deepest level of consciousness within us where our motivation for actions is engendered. "But the things that come out of the mouth come from the heart, and it is these that make a man unclean" (Mt 15:18). The vessel had to be cleansed from within and the first step to that cleansing was an inner attentiveness to the thoughts. Jesus knew that, where our thoughts are, there will be our treasure (Lk 12:34).

Paul describes the spiritual life in terms of a struggle, a battle, a warfare engaged against spiritual forces that seek one's destruction. The aim is to seek always the will of God out of loving submission to him. But this means to enter into the lists, the arena, and stand courageously against the attacks of the evil forces (Eph 6:10-13).

Putting on the mind of Jesus Christ

Besides the negative therapy that is part of spiritual *praxis,* there is more importantly the positive aspect of developing the virtues necessary to live as divinized children of God. Putting on the virtues that Jesus lived in his earthly life is, therefore, a necessary part of spiritual discipline that frees us from our sinful self. We imitate Jesus (Mt 11:29-30) as the most powerful motive for living as free children of God.

Asceticism for modern Christians must primarily consist in a gentle spirit that listens attentively to God's Spirit revealing that God is in this moment in-breaking with his infinite love. This inner attentiveness is what the Fathers of the desert called *nepsis,* from the Greek word *nepo,* which means to be sober, not inebriated. It refers to a mental sobriety, a mental balance, an internal disposition of inner attention to God's Spirit leading the Christian to true discernment of how a divinized child of God, rooted in the "mind of Christ," would act. This is a process of becoming free by ultimately always choosing to do the good according to God's Logos. This is the sign of divinization and true integration according to the likeness of God, brought about by fidelity to the interior living Word of God within the individual Christian.

Unceasing prayer

Prayer is not only one of the manifestations of the spiritual life and the measure of how divinized an individual has become, but it is the spiritual life itself. It is when we in our weakness do not know how to pray as we ought, that the Spirit comes to our weakness and prays in us (Rm 8:26-27). Real prayer is when one no longer says prayers to an extrinsic God, but when the Christian "becomes" prayer and makes his or her life the unceasing communion with God. When the prayer is purified and becomes unceasing, then it makes every act, thought and word of the individual a sign of the divine presence.

Prayer stretches to the ultimate stage on earth when divinization is revealed as the vision of divine light, the so-called *Taboric light* of the Eastern Christian tradition, in which the Christian receives an inner illumination of being bathed in the radiance of the indwelling Trinity which is shared by the divinized child of God.

Thus divinization, as revealed in scripture and tradition, is the work of the Holy Spirit together with the Son as love for the Father. This love dwells within the Christian, loving the Christian infinitely as the Father loves the Son and the Spirit. "As the Father has loved me, so I have loved you" (Jn 15:9).

The greatest mystery of God is his Trinity. He is the Father, the Son and the Holy Spirit, one God in three persons. According to 1 John 4:17, we are already becoming "as he is," and, according to 1 John 3:2, in the *eschaton* "we shall be like him, because we shall see him as he really is," which means we shall see and we shall be like the triune God. But how do we become like God: the Father, the Son and the Holy Spirit? And even in this life on earth?

The answer is given by John and Paul. According to the words of Jesus in John 3:6, the person who "is born of the Spirit is spirit." Then we can become like the Holy Spirit. We know that through the rebirth in baptism we become, not only like the Spirit, but also like the Son, not by nature, but by adoption through grace (Rm 8:14-17; Ga 4:4-7; 1 Jn 3:2). When we are born of the Spirit, we are called to become one with Christ. "I live now not I, but Christ lives in me" (Ga 2:20).

There is no better way for us to conclude this chapter on divinization than to quote the words of Jesus: "Father, may they all be one in us, as you are in me and I am in you" (Jn 17:21). Divinization is the perfect fulfillment of his prayer. It is also the fulfillment of this unity in the *eschaton* or the life hereafter that Paul describes:

And when everything is subjected to him, then
the Son himself will be subject in his turn to
the one who subjected all things to him, so that
God may be all in all. (1 Co 15:28)

Notes

1. These are the words of Basil as quoted in the burial sermon by Gregory of Nazianzen: *Oratio in laudem Basilii Magni; Oratio* 43 (*PG* 36.560A).
2. Johannine texts abound. Cf: Jn 1:3, 12-13; 3:5, 15-16, 19, 36; 5:26; 6:35, 39, 63; 7:39; 10:34; 14:15, 20; 15:1-9, 23; 17:21-23, 26; 1 Jn 1:15; 3:2, 9; 4:8-17.
3. Irenaeus, *Adversus Haereses,* bk. 5, Preface (*PG* 7.1120).
4. Athanasius, *Ad Adelphium* (*PG* 26.5898).
5. Clement of Alexandria, *Protrepticos* 1.8, in Paul Evdokimov, *Orthodoxie* (Neuchatel, 1965), 113.
6. Basil, "Man received order to become God," *De Spiritu Sancto* (*PG* 32.698) and Pseudo-Macarius, *Homilies* 1:2, 3 and 45.
7. Maximus the Confessor's words, without the identification of nature, are in Greek: "choris tes kai ousian tautoteta," see *PG* 91.1308B.
8. O. Clement, *Sur la Pentecote,* in *Contacts* (1971), 23:276.
9. Symeon the New Theologian, *Hymns of Divine Love,* trans. G. A. Maloney (Denville: Dimension Books, 1976), 50.254 (hereafter *Hymns*).
10. Cf: Paul Evdokimov, *L'Esprit Saint dans la tradition orthodoxe* (Paris: Cerf, 1969), 97.
11. Basil, *De Spiritu Sancto* (*PG* 32.133C). Cf. my article, "Epiclesis," *The New Catholic Encyclopedia (NCE)* (New York: McGraw-Hill, 1967) 5:464-466.
12. Cf. my booklet, *Following Jesus in the Real World: Asceticism Today* (Albany: Clarity Publishing, 1979).

Chapter 7

Jesus Christ Dwells Within You

If the twentieth and twenty-first centuries can be characterized in a few words from our human viewpoint, we must admit that they are characterized mainly as an intensive search of who the individual is as a unique individual, a person. Experimental and in-depth psychology, psychiatry, psycho-analysis, phenomenology, para-psychology, down to the mind-expanding courses of yoga, Silva mind control, TM, *est*, transactional analysis and so forth all bear witness to our modern search, no longer outside in nature and in the world of doing to find identity and fulfillment, but inside of one's psyche.

Into ourselves we plunge to undergo the most fascinating journey through inner space. Dangers rear up out of the dark shadows of yesteryears' repressed experiences. Shakespeare reminds us that all of us "in his time plays many parts. His acts being seven ages."[1] Carl Jung assures us that "individuation means becoming a single, homogeneous being, and, insofar as 'individuality' embraces our innermost, last and incomparable uniqueness, it also implies becoming one's own self. We could therefore translate individuation as 'coming to selfhood' or 'self-realization.' "[2]

Who are you?

The process of discovering who you are in your own uniqueness as an individual demands passing beyond the superficial levels of your own controlled consciousness in order to pass into the innermost core of your being. Great discipline is demanded for this. Silence and aloneness with the transcendent absolute are necessary. But as you pass through various layers of psychic experiences, danger zones rear up. The voyager into the interior passes into waters filled with hidden rocks ready to capsize the small sailing vessel. Repressed material that has been drowned in the unconscious can rise threateningly to disturb such a pilgrim into inner space.

William B. Yeats describes well how we moderns seek to distract ourselves from such confrontation with our "dread" self:

> The child pursuing lizards in the grass,
> The sage, who deep in central nature delves,
> The preacher watching for the evil hour to pass,
> All these are souls that fly from their dread selves.[3]

Although most of us believe that the superficial "self," which Carl Jung calls the *persona* is our true self, there lies even beyond this, reached through the long process called "individuation," our true self. We need to live in paradox and antinomy, in light and darkness at the same time, in dying and rising. This we fear for we like the security where everything is clear to us, all is daylight, distinct and not fuzzy to our intellect. In such pseudo-security we think we are in complete control. We must, however, make a choice, if we are to find our true self, in the words of Yeats, not

> to destroy
> All those antinomies
> Of day and night. . . .[4]

We must be ready to push beyond the illusion of unity in our superficial "self" to seek an integration of personality or of wholeness of person that needs the healing power of the divine Absolute. Hermann Hesse puts it in his *Steppenwolf*, that, though it appears to be an inborn and imperative need of all human beings to regard the superficial self as a true unity, yet daring persons of genius "break through the illusion of the unity of the personality and perceive that the self is made up of a bundle of selves. . . ."[5] It is the search for that true self which lies beyond the bundle of selves that prayerful encounter with God as love is all about.

Jesus—the way to our true self

Christianity reveals clearly what an honest examination of our own human lives would reveal, namely, that as Paul writes, there is sin in our members (Rm 7:20). We are born with an inherited bias toward self in false pride and love. We cannot effect our own integration without the power of the Divine Physician, the Master Psychiatrist, Jesus Christ. He has the fullness of life in himself, the true image of the invisible God (1 Co 1:15).

It is only through the Holy Spirit that we can know the full Jesus Christ and our true selves in loving oneness with him. "We know that he lives in us by the Spirit that he has given us" (1 Jn 3:24). The work of the Spirit is to make us holy or sanctified as we live more consistently, not only as Jesus lived in complete submission in all things to his Father, but all with Jesus living in us. Our "individuation" into the fully integrated human being you and I should become by God's unique love for each of us can be realized only by the interacting, loving relationships of the Father, Son and Holy Spirit toward us in inner intimacy.

Let us develop in this chapter the important subject of the indwelling presence of Jesus Christ within us. But we must keep in mind the inseparability of the Son and the Father. The Holy Spirit is also always present, uniting them into their loving oneness and uniqueness.

Too good to believe

There are many truths in Christianity to which we give lip service or a head-knowledge consent, yet if we were to live by them, such revealed truths would radically change our lives. One such truth is that a Christian in the state of grace possesses the risen, glorified Jesus Christ. By living constantly our baptism of dying to self, the words of Paul apply to us: "You have died and now the life you have is hidden with Christ in God" (Col 3:3). Paul continuously speaks of the Christian who must put on Jesus Christ (Ga 3:27; Eph 4:24) and live *in* Christ.

The truth of Jesus dwelling within us is revealed through the incarnation of God's Son as human, his teachings, healings and miracles, recorded in the gospels, through his death on the cross, resurrection and outpouring of his Holy Spirit (1 Jn 3:24).

If our faith assures us that God is love and wishes to live most intimately within our very being, then what prevents us from experiencing this reality as a constant state? He came among us to make it possible, not only that we might become children of God, but that at all times we might live in that continued awareness discovered in each moment of our lives. This is our human dignity: to be called children of God, and we really are such (1 Jn 3:1) in the process of discovering and surrendering to the uncreated energies of God living within you and within the context of each human situation or event. God is saying in substance to you: "Here I am; this place is holy. Take off your shoes, your securities, and approach this burning bush to become consumed by the fire of my divine love for you."

The secret of our continued growth in prayer and the Christian spiritual journey is one of growing in greater and greater degrees of awareness and conscious experience of God's immanent or indwelling presence as self-emptying love within us. How absolutely sad that Jesus Christ, God's living Word made flesh, and still revealing to us the mysteries of God through the gift of his Holy Spirit, wishes to lead us into the presence of the Holy Trinity as the source and ultimate center of all reality and, yet, we Christians in general remain ignorant of this truth.

For most of us Christians, the reality of the indwelling Trinity made possible by grace through Jesus Christ and his Spirit remains a supernatural mystery beyond our human knowledge and understanding. Therefore, it has usually for us no "practical" impact on our daily lives. It simply is a mystery not to be understood and therefore not to be experienced!

Our human dignity

This is the incomparably "good news": Jesus Christ, true God and true man, who has died freely out of love for each of us, but is risen, now lives within us. We are, in the words of Ignatius of Antioch (c +115), Christbearers (*christophoroi*). The kingdom of God is truly within us! What amazing love God has for each of us in that he has given us his only-begotten Son (Jn 3:16), who in the flesh was able to die for love of us in order to image the infinite love that the Father has for each one of us.

In his risen existence the full Jesus Christ, God-man, can now be in us and we, by his Holy Spirit, can be in him. This is God's greatest gift, the Spirit, unseparated from the risen Christ, yet distinct. The two personalized relations within the Trinity are communicated to the Christian. This gift contains both Jesus Christ and the Holy Spirit, who have their full being in relationship to the Father.

Do you understand the dignity to which you are called? Do you understand how beautiful you really are, right now, in spite of your brokenness, past sinfulness and self-centeredness, in the Trinity's indwelling love for you? This is the good news that the Word made flesh makes possible through his Spirit, who reveals to us in each moment that Jesus dwells within us and with him the Father and the bonding into a oneness through the Holy Spirit.

Paul must have been carried away many times as he understood that this Jesus Christ, who died for him out of a personal love (Ga 2:20), also lived within him. He calls this "the mystery of Christ" (Eph 3:4). This experiential knowledge was given him as a gift of faith and he burned to communicate a share in that faith-revelation to all he met. He wished to be a Jew to the Jew, weak to the weak, to win all to Christ (1 Co 9:20-22). Paul had accepted the loss of everything in order to live in the indwelling Christ. Everything else he considered rubbish so long as he can have Christ (Ph 3:9). His one prayer is: "All I want is to know Christ and the power of his resurrection and to share his sufferings by reproducing the pattern of his death (Ph 3:10).

To live in Christ

Paul received the central doctrine of Christianity concerning our "incorporation" into Christ's own life, into his very own being, from Christ himself. We understood that to live the new life of eternal life, we must consider ourselves dead to sin, but "alive to God in Christ Jesus" (Rm 6:11). We must be united *with* Christ. We must be *in* Christ.

This phrase is used 164 times by Paul to express a very real, intimate union with the indwelling Christ.

Baptism puts us into direct contact with the resurrected, glorified Christ who now, by his spiritualized body-person, can come and truly dwell within us. The "new man" is precisely this given individual, baptized in Christ, now living according to the new inner principle of life which Christ is. It is truly "Christ who lives in me" (Ga 2:20). We, baptized into the trinitarian life, become adopted children of God through Jesus Christ who incorporates us into his human-divine being (Ga 4:5, 3:26). We become aware that we live in a relationship similar to that which exists between God the Father and his only-begotten Son, Jesus Christ, because the same life of the Son is dwelling within us.

In baptism we become inserted into Christ, he the head, we his members: "Now the Church is his body, he is its head" (Col 1:18). We become true sons and daughters of the heavenly Father (son, *huios:* Rm 8:14, 19; 9:26; 2 Co 6:18; Ga 3:26; 4:7) through divine adoption *(huiothesia)* by which we become heirs of heavenly, eternal divine life in Christ of the Father (Rm 8:15; Ga: 4:5; Eph 1:5).

Transformation into the image of Christ

The relationship to Christ brought about by baptism is more than a mere extrinsic, ethical model to be imitated by us. We Christians are to live in the most vital union with Jesus, who lives within us as the principle of all our thoughts, words and actions. Augustine captured the meaning of Paul in the daring affirmation which Pope Paul, in his encyclical, *Ecclesiam Suam*, applied to us modern Christians:

> Let us rejoice and give thanks that we have become not only Christians, but Christ. My brothers, do you understand the grace of God our Head? Stand in admiration, rejoice; we have become Christ.[6]

Maximus the Confessor of the seventh century well describes this great mystery of the indwelling Christ as Christ transforming us Christians by being born spiritually within us:

The Word of God, born once in the flesh (such is his kindness and goodness), is always willing to be born spiritually in those who desire him. In them he is born as an infant as he fashions himself in them by means of their virtues. He reveals himself to the extent that he knows someone is capable of receiving him. He diminishes the revelation of his glory, not out of selfishness, but because he recognizes the capacity and resources of those who desire to see him. Yet, in the transcendence of mystery, he always remains invisible to all.[7]

The Christian shares in Christ's own life, that life of the historical person, Jesus Christ, now gloriously resurrected. He is personally incorporated into Christ, without losing one's own identity. Christ lives in us, but he must always be further formed in us (Ga 4:19). By our yielding to the life-giving influence of Christ, we are gradually transformed into the image and likeness of Christ.

The first creation of Adam according to the image of God (Gn 1:26-28), as understood by Paul, is a mere shadow, a symbol, of the true likeness to which God has predestined all human beings in the order of salvation through intimate union with the Son and Holy Spirit. The only destiny God ever had conceived for all of us human beings is our transformation into the image and likeness of the only-begotten Son, Jesus Christ. "For those he has foreknown he has also predestined to be conformed to the image of his Son, so that this Son should be the first-born among many brothers" (Rm 8:29).

For Paul, the doctrine of the incorporation of the Christian in Christ and transfiguration into him through his grace and our cooperation, were nothing esoteric, no delicacy reserved for a select few. In Paul's teaching, as we Christians turn away from our sinful pasts in a true *metanoia* or conversion of our whole being to God, we enter into a permanent union of life *in* and *with* Christ. One is a Christian only so long as he or she lives in this union with Christ. One may not experience feelings or even sensible awareness of this union with Christ, but these are not essential to the reality.

Possessed by Christ

This reality we attain by faith as the Savior himself said before his ascension: "He that believes and is baptized, will be saved" (Mt 16:16). Neither the mere external example of Christ, derived from the gospels, nor his ideas operate on us in some vague, impersonal way. The very historical person of Jesus who indwells in us as a spirit, yet personal power, this is the Christian dynamic. To be baptized in Christ is to be possessed by his living person as risen.

Paul was "apprehended" by Christ (Ph 3:2), so that the principle of his every thought, word and deed was no longer merely Paul, the natural man, subjected to the laws of the flesh, but Christ, "who lives in me" (Ga 2:20). It is the Christ who has died on the cross and has risen from the dead, the Christ of history, who lives in him and also in us.

Paul seized on the reality of this relationship to Christ and never tired of seeking different metaphors to bring out its vivid truth. He speaks of the life of Christ within the Christian as a new life that must be put on, not by some few, but by all Christians.

> You are, in fact, all children of God through faith in Jesus Christ, since all of you who have come to Christ by baptism have clothed yourselves with Christ. No longer is there Jew or Greek; no longer is there slave or freeman; no longer is there male or female. You are all one in Christ Jesus. (Ga 3:27-28)

To "put on Christ" is to become surrounded by him, penetrated by his living presence and activity as indwelling the Christian. This relation to Christ is not merely a moral union. It is real, ontological, of two persons, Christ Jesus and the individual Christian, united by the Spirit of God's love into an intimate union which, however, allows for the differentiated uniqueness of each person.

Growth in Jesus Christ

But Christ's presence within us must grow as an embryo grows in the womb. Paul wanted to spend himself in order that his Galatian Christians might grow up into Christ. "My dear children, I am again suffering the pangs of childbirth for you, until Christ is formed within you" (Ga 4:19).

This divine-human life of Christ admits of growth within us, dependent on our cooperation. From the embryonic life given to us in baptism we are to progress unto "perfect manhood, to the mature measure of the fullness of Christ" (Eph 4:13). Again, Paul, shows this growth as a progress in unity of faith and deeper knowledge of the Son of God, whereby we come to know "what is the breadth and length and height and depth and to know Christ's love which surpasses knowing, in order that . . . we may be perfected and bring to realization God's fullness" (Eph 3:18-19).

The effect of this ontological union with Christ is the activation in the individual Christian's life of a piety and conduct of life similar to that of Christ's life. We, raised to a new life by possessing a new principle of activity, Christ himself, must not merely possess this life, but must "walk in the newness of life" (Rm 6:4).

Intrinsic to this process of putting on Christ is that we already possess, as a seed possesses the future tree, the final goal, but not yet. Paul, depending on his view of the process, which is defined by its goal, can say that we have been already saved (Eph 2:5, 8), while, looking at the dynamic process, he can say that we are "in the process of being saved" (1 Co 1:18; 2 Co 2:15).

Hence, the Christian life in Christ is precisely a continuous process of despoiling oneself of all self-love, of casting off the "outward man" in order to renew constantly the "inward man" (2 Co 4:16), so as to grow into the fullness of Christ. The difference in the degrees of virtues will be more evident when we view the community growth in Christ wherein exist simultaneously individuals of varying degrees of Christian perfection in the same body of Christ, the Church. This we will point out is the work of the Holy Spirit to bring each Christian into the "new sphere of life" (Rm 6:4) which the Spirit creates. Christians are not only to be *christophoroi*, Christbearers, but they were also to be *pneumatikoi*, spiritualized by the Spirit, whose primary function in the Christian's life is to be recognized concretely in the creation of this life in Christ which flows out to build up the total Christ, he the head and all Christians the living members in him.

Light and darkness coexisting

This is the awesome dignity brought about by God's primal grace, the triune persons as uncreated energies of love, elevating us into becoming sharers with them of their divine nature (2 P 1:4) through the created relationship that we call *sanctifying grace* to be in union with Jesus Christ by his Spirit so that the Father looks upon us and loves us as incorporated into his only Son, Jesus Christ. This is the mystery hidden for centuries that has now been revealed to his saints (Col 1:27-28).

Yet how we are called to walk with humility and purity of heart since we have not yet reached the goal, the fullness of our life in Christ! We live both in inner darkness and in the radiant light of the indwelling persons of the Trinity. You and I become light in the night of our brokenness and sinful roots that lie so deeply encrusted in the inner reaches of even our unconscious. How can darkness receive within itself a light and, without being dissipated by the light, still remain somehow in the middle of the light?

Symeon the New Theologian maintains this mystery in paradoxical, antimonical language:

> O awesome wonder which I see doubly,
> with my two sets of eyes, of the body and of the soul!
> Listen now; I am telling you the awesome mysteries
> Of a double God who came to me as to a double man.
> He took upon himself my flesh and he gave me his Spirit.
> And I became also god by divine grace,
> A son of God, but by adoption.
> O what dignity, what glory![8]

A greater than I

Gabriel Marcel, the French philosopher, writes about this basic urge in all human beings to plunge deeper into oneself to find the true self in someone else. "I can be led to recognize that deep down in me there is something other than me, something further within me than I am myself."[9]

Inside of you, beyond the swirling of the outside world of so much rapid movement, disharmony and threatening chaos there is the core of your being, where your *I-ness* is continually being birthed into your true self through the center of peace and power, healing love and strength. This center is the indwelling Jesus Christ that you can touch intimately through faith, hope and love and be touched by his infinite love, one with the love of the Father and Holy Spirit.

Christ is the center of the world and yet resides at your center as in his temple. He is the Alpha and the Omega, "who is, who was, and who is to come, the Almighty" (Rv 1:8). Jesus risen stands as light shining in our brokenness and whispers from the depths of our being:

> Do not be afraid; it is I, the First and the Last; I am the Living One, I was dead and now I am to live for ever and ever, and I hold the keys of death and of the underworld. (Rv 1:17-18)

Christ within us is light that dissipates the darkness. To be a Christian is to become ever more aware that Christ lives in us. It is to live in a oneness with him. It is to receive his constant love that showed itself on the cross, but that was captured forever in the risen Christ. If there is the darkness of sin, we must struggle to dissipate such darkness. Sin in any form is the absence of the life of Christ in our lives.

But fighting the negative elements cannot be the sole aim of our life. It is in removing them or better in having such negativity transformed so the positive focus of true Christianity can be accentuated. And this means to live in the reality that the risen Christ lives within us through his Spirit. We truly are now part of God's family insofar as we exist totally in Christ. This entails great inner discipline in order that Christ be the norm of all our thoughts, words and deeds (2 Co 10:5-8).

True love is obedience to God's Word

Obedience to Christ is the index of our love for him and of our union with him. Such loving submission demands the free sacrifice of our own wills, in the sense of our autonomous, compulsive, self-centered wills that we close off from the illumination of Christ's Spirit and the discovery of our true self in Christ.

Love of Christ and union with him is impossible without obedience on our part which unites our will with his. This is a freely chosen, spontaneous act that is done sheerly out of love and never out of fear or coercion. Thus we can see that the indwelling Christ within us brings about an intimate union of our will with that of Christ, which union of wills expresses itself in the way of life lived in love of God and neighbor.

While reading the Fathers of the desert, I have often been impressed by the fact that the one work they assigned to all Christians, regardless of their state of life, is to observe Christ's commandments. We hear from Christ himself that, if we truly love him, we will keep his word ". . . and my Father will love him, and we shall come to him and make our home with him" (Jn 14:23). Obeying Christ's word is more than observing the Ten Commandments. It comes down to a state of listening to the indwelling Christ as he, through his Spirit, reveals to the Christian the mind of the Father in each event.

Often the Christian mystics, especially of the Greek-speaking East, used the symbol of seeing Christ within themselves as light, illuminating their minds as to what was the will of God in the given moment. The end of the incarnation is precisely that God's divine life may be restored within our inner being by Jesus Christ, entering within our spiritual faculties by grace. We should desire hungrily to possess this inner presence of Jesus as light in a more conscious, unifying way. As we grow in deeper silencing of our "heart" and begin to see how bound we are by shadow and darkness, by sense pleasures and false values, in such a state of alienation, we cry continually to see more of Christ's light, to experience more and more his assimilating presence that will bridge the abyss that separates our sinful selves from him in a union of loving surrender. Jesus Christ, the Light of the world, makes himself "seen within us."

The light from within

No one alone can reach this level of seeing Jesus Christ within. No spiritual director can teach another how to reach this state of living in the light of Christ. Only the indwelling Trinity can reveal it to us in experience. Jesus often referred to himself as light, especially in John's gospel. "I, the light, have come into the world, so that whoever believes in me need not stay in the dark any more" (Jn 12:46). Our growth in perfection consists in the intensity of union that we attain through the conscious awareness of Jesus Christ living in us with the resulting surrender totally of ourselves in a perfect *symbiosis* or a life together of two wills operating as one through the union brought about by the Spirit. The life of Christ grows as we yield to his real presence within us, as we cooperate with him in all of our thoughts and actions.

Jesus Christ tells us that he lives in us with the Father and the Spirit. He is light. His personalized presence shines day and night within our hearts, illuminating our intelligence. It bathes us in his radiance and knows no setting. It draws us into the same life-giving and transforming light. This manner of speaking, at least among the Eastern Christian Fathers, that Christ is light is to say that he is sensed as present and acting in a loving, transforming manner. It is not in a sensible way as seen with our physical eyes, but we become aware of him in an intelligible manner through contemplation.

Symeon the New Theologian summarizes well the consistent teaching of the Eastern Fathers on the indwelling Christ within the Christian as light:

> O immensity of ineffable glory, O excess of love! He who contains all things dwells in the interior of a corrupt and mortal man, whose every possession is in the power of him who inhabits him. Man indeed becomes truly like a woman carrying a child. O stupendous prodigy, of an incomprehensible God, works and mysterious incomprehensible! A man bears consciously in himself God as light, him who has produced and created all things, holding even the man who carries him. Man carries him interiorly as a treasure which transcends words, written or spoken, any quality, quantity, image, matter and figure, shaped in an inexplicable beauty, all entirely simple as light, he who transcends all light.[10]

A transfiguring light

As we are bathed in the transfiguring power of the indwelling Jesus, we are able to release the same transfiguring presence of Jesus in the world around us. He "fills the whole creation" (Eph 1:23). Sharing in his priesthood through our baptism, we can release the risen Lord and ask him to transform each person we meet, each material thing we touch, to bring God's kingdom into being "on earth as it is in heaven."

What a power we Christian contemplatives have to call forth the transforming power of Jesus Christ into our modern world, one that groans so loudly in agony until the full Christ is born. Such Christians live in a paschal hope that, although alone we are completely weak, however, with Jesus Christ within us, we can do all things in him who strengthens us (2 Co 12:9). We cry out at all times that the body of Christ, the total Christ, will be fashioned out of all the material elements that pass through our lives, "Come, Lord Jesus, Marana tha!" (Rv 22:20).

Fiery prayer

As we yearn ardently in moments of restful contemplation or in our busy work during the day to become more united with God through Christ in his Spirit, our prayer ignites into a longing for God that nothing created can ever satisfy. St. Isaac of Nineveh describes such contemplative prayer:

> Your heart is aflame, burns like fire day and night; and so the whole world seems to you like dust and dung; you even have no desire for food, for the sweetness of new flaming thoughts, constantly arising in your soul. Suddenly fountains of tears open up in you, flowing freely like an inexhaustible stream and mingling with all your activities, with your reading, your prayer or meditation, your eating or drinking or aught else. When you see this in your soul, be of good cheer, for you have crossed the sea. Then be diligent in your work, stand watchfully on guard, that grace may increase in you from day to day.[11]

Returning to the market place

Having plunged deeply into oneself, the Christian contemplative has begun to be transformed into Christ. It is not an absorption or assimilation of the human personhood into Christ. It is the peak of divine love that has brought such Christians to a realization of the end for which they have been created: to be in the likeness of Jesus Christ. This union with Christ floods the contemplatives with deep repose and interior joy. They sense an inner harmony of having arrived at fulfillment in Christ.

And yet such Christians experience God's unique love poured out also upon every creature. The Christ within them sends them forth to become mediators to the world. Such contemplatives, having received God's Word, like the prophets of old, are driven by the Spirit to share that Word, Jesus Christ, with the world. They know from scripture that real love of God is linked to genuine, active love of neighbor. But they know it now by an inner knowledge of oneness with Christ within themselves and a oneness with the total Christ outside themselves.

As God is "toward" them in self-giving through Jesus in his Spirit, so they now intuit both the ideal oneness between themselves and all human beings in Christ. But they also intuit the estrangement of many from that oneness. They suffer the sufferings of Christ to bring the lost sheep into the one fold. They burn with the love of Christ in them that urges them to spend their energies in loving service to others. The silent listening to the indwelling Christ awakens a deeper sense of awareness of the divine intelligence working within the depths of their being. They experience easily a greater good and inner meaning and relationship of all creatures being rooted ultimately in God as the ground of their being.

They learn how to respond in harmony with God's promptings. Such praying in the heart brings about an inner tension that can never be done away with. They are one in peace and harmony with the indwelling Christ and yet burn with an insatiable hunger to be more dissolved with Paul to be more intimately united with Christ. They also burn with a restless zeal to bring Christ into the lives of others who are unaware of the promises of Christ to dwell within them as in his temple.

We see these hungers in the life of Catherine of Siena where all are subsumed in one word: *desire.* Catherine of Siena reports in her *Dia-*

logues the saying of Christ: "I am infinite Good and I therefore require of you infinite desire."[12]

Authentic test of Christianity

The power of true Christianity lies in holding out to all of us an active participation in the inner life and love of the triune God. We reach our true identity to the degree that we live in Christ, that he and we form a oneness in active love. We can never be in doubt as to how intense is our union with Christ. It is measured by our surrender to the indwelling Christ, who directs us through his Spirit outwardly to be his "ambassadors" and "reconcilers" with him of the world (2 Co 5:18-19). We know the abiding power of Christ loving within us by the love we show to others.

> If we love one another, God dwells in us and his love is perfected in us . . . and we have known and believed the love that God has for us. God is love; and he that dwells in love dwells in God and God in him. (1 Jn 4:12, 16)

The love-energy of Christ operates in us in all of our human relationships. The same Christ, that imaged the love of the heavenly Father by dying for us and for the whole world, lives within us. As we yield to his loving, transforming presence, one with him, the gentle, meek, compassionate, suffering Servant of Yahweh, we move with him to serve the world in order to bring it into his very own body to the glory of the Trinity. Love toward others and humble service determine the intensity of our union with Jesus Christ. Our uniqueness as persons is likewise measured by love and service in humility toward others. These are the signs that we are not only vibrant Christians, but fully realized human beings, made according to the image and likeness of Jesus Christ who dwells within us.

Practical resolutions

By way of summarizing the content of this chapter, I would like to append some practical resolutions to help the reader move this fundamental teaching of the indwelling Jesus Christ within each Christian by grace into the realm of the living out of this truth in the practical details of one's daily life.

1. The beginning and continued orientation from darkness to live in the light of Christ dwelling within you is that you be firmly persuaded by God's revealed words in scripture and the teaching of the Church the Jesus Christ, God-man, truly lives in all his transcendent light and power within you. He has already taken the initiative. It is for you to wish to respond to this reality of the indwelling Christ as light within you. Joy, thanksgiving, adoration, but—above all—worship and complete surrender of yourself to Christ and his Father in the Spirit of love that inundates you continually with this interior knowledge of God's presence as intimate and active love abiding within you at all times are part of your response.

2. To induce a more complete surrender to Christ's inner guidance, entertain always a passionate desire to be in most intimate oneness with Jesus and to surrender your whole being to him in loving obedience.

3. Strive to increase the faith, hope and love that have been infused into you in your baptism. Rooted in God's revelation concerning his transcendence, his nature as love and self-giving and through the risen Lord Jesus his immanence as indwelling within you, you turn inwardly to a different level than the habitual, busy, doing level of your ordinary consciousness. This other level can co-exist as another level of consciousness that can become stronger and stronger as God's infusion of faith, hope and love becomes stronger. Develop a spirit of interior recollection based on divine teaching to seek throughout the day in thoughts, words and deeds

to realize the abiding presence of Christ within you. "He must increase; I must decrease" (Jn 3:30).

4. Try to live in a *synergy* (a working together) with the Lord by doing everything in closest union and desire with him. Seek to do all *with, in,* and *for* Jesus Christ. Not your will be done, but his.

5. Without strain, seek throughout the day to practice affective aspirations to purify your intentions to do all for God's glory. At times it may be a simple sigh, an act of love and self-surrender to the risen Lord living within you. Let his name and his presence be on your lips and in your heart.

6. When you may have failed to live in such a loving union, be quick to humble yourself in sensitive sorrow and firm resolution to return to a loving oneness with the Lord.

7. Be constantly vigilant not to allow any self-centeredness in thought, word or deed to take you away from Christ-centeredness.

8. Seek to put on the mind of Jesus by a continued desire to love the heavenly Father with your whole heart, one with the heart of Jesus. Love the Father as Jesus loves him through the Spirit.

9. Finally, instead of seeing all things in and through your own desires and understanding, adopt the vast interests and burning love of Jesus for the entire world. Love the uniqueness of each of God's creatures as a special participated manifestation of something of God's infinite goodness and beauty in matter, especially in your respect and love for all human beings who share with you in the very imageness and likeness of Jesus Christ. Move away in your spiritual life from an ego-centric piety to a pan-cosmic oneness with God's creatures. Live only to be Christ's ambassador, to be a co-creator with him of a new creation (2 Co 5:18).

Conclusion

This is the great truth that Jesus Christ has come to reveal to us and make possible in a continued growth in consciousness of our intimate union with him and through him to live already in the kingdom of heaven which is the indwelling Trinity within each of us as Christians. The inner light of Christ leads you into the light of the indwelling Trinity which suffuses your entire being as you joyfully experience in every thought, word and deed the exhilarating joy of being a child of God. God has called you "out of darkness into his wonderful light" (1 P 2:9).

But the light of Christ within you is to shine through you outward toward others and all of God's creatures. "In the same way your light must shine in the sight of men, so that, seeing your good works, they may give the praise to your Father in heaven" (Mt 5:16). You now have the power, to the degree that you have become light from Christ's indwelling light within you, to bring the same transfiguring light to the world that lies in darkness and brokenness and self-centeredness all around you.

Christ can become light for them only if you and like-minded Christians allow his light of love to go through you into the darkness of others. You breathe the name of Jesus and his light-presence over each person you meet. You believe, as you have experienced within yourself, that they also can rise to a sharing in his risen glory and become less dark and more of loving light in the world.

I Surrender

I pray alone
on the mountaintops of night.
It is so calm, so still.
All is dark;
yet coming closer and closer
to me is a robe
of great brilliance.
I close my eyes in fear.
As the full Sun,

he stops before me,
dazzling, dancing.
His presence pierces
through my whole being
like fire searing, burning,
yet consuming me not.
I kiss the earth before Brilliance
I let go and fly to ecstasy.
Oh, God, before such beauty
I surrender.

G. A. M.

Notes

1. William Shakespeare, *As You Like It,* in *The Complete Works,* ed. G. B. Harrison (New York: Harcourt, Brace & Co., 1948), 11:142-43.
2. Carl G. Jung, *The Basic Writings,* ed. Violet Staub de Laszlo (New York: Pantheon Books, Inc., 1959), 143.
3. W. B. Yeats, "Life," in *The Variorum Edition of the Poems of W. B. Yeats,* ed. Peter Allt and Russell K. Alspach (New York: The Macmillan Co., 1957).
4. *Ibid.,* in the poem, "Vacillation."
5. Hermann Hesse, *Steppenwolf,* trans. Basil Creighton (New York: Henry Hold & Co., 1978), 78.
6. Pope Paul VI, *Ecclesiam Suam* (New York: Paulist Press, 1965), 30.
7. Maximus the Confessor, *Century* I, 8-13 (*PG* 90.1182-86).
8. Symeon the New Theologian, *Hymns,* 24.136.
9. Gabriel Marcel, *The Mystery of Being,* trans. Rene Hague (Chicago: H. Regnery Co., 1960), 56.
10. Symeon the New Theologian, *Traites Ethiques,* trans. Jean Darrouzes, in *Sources Chretiénnes Series* (Paris: Cerf, 1967), vol. 129, 11, 167-77, pp. 340-42.
11. Isaac of Nineveh, *Directions on Spiritual Training,* in *Early Fathers from the Philokalia,* trans. E. Kadloubovsky & G. Palmer (London: Faber & Faber, 1954), 243.
12. Catherine of Siena, *The Dialogues,* trans. Suzanne Noffke (New York: Paulist Press, 1980), chap. 104, p.197.

Chapter 8

Transformation through the Holy Spirit

From my earliest childhood I have always been fascinated by butterflies. What beauty and grace as such a creature of God danced merrily from flower to flower, drunk with the sweetness of just being alive, in a frenzied dance of joyous abandonment! In school I learned about the butterfly's humble origins from a lowly caterpillar, not very beautiful to behold, so slow in its crawling efforts to get somewhere. The beautiful butterfly was being formed, even as a caterpillar, but even more so as the caterpillar spun its prison-like confinement and entered into the chrysalis stage. In such womb-tomb confinement, slowly, a new and more beautiful creature was being fashioned.

As the cocoon splits down its sides and the butterfly emerges, wings, wet and tightly packed, stretch out and the butterfly flies off—a new creation that hardly resembles the caterpillar. Yet all that beauty and ability to fly were locked in hidden potential within the ugly little caterpillar. I later learned in college biology that those very wings were already present in outline form and basic structure in the caterpillar and pupa stages. Yet a slow metamorphosis or transformation was needed to manifest externally what was already there internally.

This for me has always been a guiding example of the transformation that can take place in the lives of all of us human beings under the power of God's creative Love, the Holy Spirit. From the moment of our conception in our mother's womb, we, too, are launched on a course of evolution. There is a bodily development that is very dependent for its full growth on outside factors, such as the genes of our parents, orienting us toward this or that type of body, of food, drink and personal loving care. But there is also in all of us a psychic and spiritual development that requires very much our own cooperation if we are to reach new levels of human perfection. God's evolving Spirit of love is operating during our earthly pilgrimage by drawing out on the physical level what has been locked inside of the 100,000 genes in the twenty-three pairs of chromosomes in conception. The physical genes received gratuitously through our blood line dispose us to a continued development guided by God's creative, loving power. This growth will evolve hidden potentials of psychic and spiritual abilities that in our finitude will never know the possibility of stopping an enriching growth, not even in the life to come, provided we individuals cooperate with God's transforming Spirit.

The Holy Spirit: the divine harmonizer

Our Christian faith assures us that God, as a trinitarian community of love, explodes in his *kenotic* or self-emptying love to create a world of seemingly infinite diversity. Yet all multiplicity is continually being guided by the loving, over-shadowing Holy Spirit to fashion a oneness, the fullness of the *Logos God* enfleshed in matter. The Spirit is moving lovingly throughout the material world to draw God's embryonic creation into the definitive unity—the body of Christ.

Athanasius in the fourth century expressed such Christian optimism in a world moving toward an ordered beauty and harmony through the Holy Spirit.

Like a musician who has attuned his lyre, and by the artistic blending of low and high and medium tones produces a single melody, so the Wisdom of God, holding the universe like a lyre, adapting things heavenly to things earthly, and earthly things to heavenly, harmonizes them all, and leading them by his will, makes one world and one world-order in beauty and harmony.[1]

Overshadowing of the Holy Spirit

From the Book of Genesis we see at the beginning of creation by the Trinity, a community of an *I-thou* in a *we* community, the presence of the Holy Spirit as God's creative power. God's presence as loving

Orderer and *Harmonizer* is seen as his Spirit of love hovering over the chaos and the world like a mighty, cosmic bird. "Now the earth was a formless void, there was darkness over the deep, and God's spirit hovered over the water" (Gn 1:1-2).

God the Father utters his creative Word by calling his Spirit down upon the cosmos in a continuous cosmic *epiclesis* (in Greek, a literal calling down upon something) to divinize matter into spirit. God breathes his breath, his *ruah,* his loving Spirit, as the principle of life into all his creation. The beasts of the land are sustained by his breath. The heavens are also the work of God's inspiriting breath, his Spirit (Gn 7:15).

But in a special way God breathes his breath into man and woman and they become human persons, capable of communicating with God, who makes them destined to share in his very own image and likeness (Gn 1:26-27). But all human beings, by the inbreathing of God's Spirit, are called to cooperate in harmonizing all of creation into a work of conscious love, a harmony of diversity in oneness through love (Gn 1:28-30).

Of all material creatures, only man and woman have free will to respond through personal choices to God's call to share in his intimate community of love through his Spirit. The necessity for decision, an obligation which we can never evade, is the distinguishing feature of us human beings. We have been created by God to reply to his call and in this answer alone to fulfill or destroy the purpose of God's creation.

A love-covenant

God becomes actively present to us and invites us into intimate union with him through his Spirit of love. It is only God's love, his Spirit, who can bring about true communion in love. When God created woman and gave her to man, he breathed his Spirit of intimate love into them and bound them together into a union, bone of his bone and flesh of his flesh (Gn 2:23). God joined them together in love and they became "one body" (Gn 2:23). Christianity would guarantee that whenever we live in love toward each other, it would be the Holy Spirit who would be perfecting the love of God on earth, enfleshing it in a new incarnation in the material world (1 Jn 4:12).

We human beings seek communion in love with God and other human beings because God is this way in his very nature as love. God the Father in absolute silence, in a communication of love impossible for us human beings to understand, speaks his one eternal Word through his Spirit of love. In that one Word, the Father is perfectly present, totally self-giving to his Son. But in his Spirit, the Father also hears his Word come back to him in a perfect, eternal yes of total surrendering love, that is again the Holy Spirit.

The Trinity is the reciprocal community of a movement of the Spirit of love between Father and Son through the Holy Spirit. The Godhead becomes real as he communicates in love with his Word. His Word gives him his identity as Father. But that means eternal self-giving to the other, his Word in love, the Holy Spirit.

The Word reveals the Spirit of love

Jesus Christ, the Word and Son of the Father made flesh out of love for us, brings us into the awesome mystery of the Trinity as a communion in its own life through his revealing Holy Spirit. From this revelation of the Holy Spirit, we can believe that the Father begets eternally his only-begotten Son through his Spirit of love. Since the Son is one in substance with the Father, he, through the incarnation, can bring us, not only to a knowledge of the Father, but he can actualize us through his Holy Spirit to become children of God sharing in his own very nature (2 P 1:4). "God became man in order that man could become God" was the constant teaching of the early Fathers, as we have already quoted.

Regeneration by the Holy Spirit

The Spirit, that the risen Jesus sends by asking his Father, is seen in the New Testament as the loving force of God himself, divinizing all who are open to receive his gift of the Spirit. This holiness, given to us to transform us into heirs of God, true children of God (Rm 8:15), is effected by the very indwelling of God's Spirit taking possession of us Christians, penetrating our minds, our thoughts, all our actions with the very life of God.

John, the beloved disciple of Jesus, cannot get over the miracle of our regeneration, ". . . not by water alone but by the Spirit" (Jn 3:3, 5). "Think of the love that the Father has lavished on us, by letting us be called God's children; and that is what we are" (1 Jn 3:1). Paul describes the main work of the Spirit as bringing us into a new life, a life in Jesus which regenerates us into true children of God: "The Spirit of God has made his home in you . . . and if the Spirit of him who raised Jesus from the dead is living in you, then he who raised Jesus from the dead will give life to your own mortal bodies through his Spirit living in you" (Rm 8:9, 11).

God's very own Spirit dwells within us as in his temple (1 Co 6:19-20). We possess through the Spirit the fullness of the triune God living and acting in love within us at all times during our waking and sleeping hours. This Spirit of love brings new life to its fullness in the proportion that we allow the Spirit to become our guide, teacher and revealer, as he guides us Christians to make choices according to the mind of Christ.

Revelation of the indwelling Spirit

That the Holy Spirit dwells within you and me is the great work of the risen Jesus. He is the expressed Word of the Father. But he would have remained a muted Word in the silence of Calvary if in his "glorification" he would not have sent his Holy Spirit, as he promised his disciples. But if we were to love him by keeping his commandments, he promised to give us the Comforter who would *abide in us.*

If you love me you will keep my commandments.
I shall ask the Father,
and he will give you another Advocate
to be with you for ever,
that Spirit of truth

who the world can never receive
since it neither sees nor knows him;
but you know him,
because he is with you, he is in you. (Jn 14:15-17)

The disciples were not to be sad by the master's leaving for if Jesus did not go, the great gift of the Spirit would not be given them (Jn 16:7). But when the Spirit of truth that proceeds from the Father comes, "He will give testimony of me" (Jn 15:27). This gift of the Spirit that would abide within the disciples was not to be given only to them "because the love of God has been poured into our hearts by the Holy Spirit which has been given us" (Rm 5:5). All of us, argues Paul, are no longer "unspiritual" but now spiritual, "since the Spirit of God has made his home in you" (Rm 8:9).

We have all been made children of God through the Holy Spirit that lives in us: "The proof that you are sons is that God has sent the Spirit of his Son into our hearts: the Spirit that cries, 'Abba, Father,' and it is this that makes you a son, you are not a slave any more" (Ga 4:6-7). This Spirit dwells in us and bears witness to our highest faculty of knowing and loving, our spirit, that we really are now God's children: "The Spirit himself and our spirit bear united witness that we are children of God" (Rm 8:16).

It has been pointed out in preceding chapters that it is the whole Trinity, Father, Son and Spirit, that comes and abides in us in a very special manner. Paul places the presence of the Spirit not only within the whole body, the Church of Christ, as he writes in 1 Colossians 3:16, but he has the Spirit as dwelling in the individual Christian.[2] This indwelling is found in his text: "Your body, you know, is the temple of the Holy Spirit, who is in you since you received him from God" (1 Co 6:19).

A special presence

What shines through such revealed texts from holy scripture is that there is a special *presence* of God, the Trinity, within the Christian through the "sending" of the Holy Spirit of Jesus and the Father. Not only is the Spirit dwelling in the hearts of the Christians, but he is there exercising a special role. We know that where one person of the Trinity is there are the other two persons. In any action of God outside of the Trinity all three persons concur in the action since they possess the same nature. Now we see the importance of the Greek Fathers' distinction between the essence of the Godhead, that is non-communicable to creatures, and his uncreated energies of love, that is the entire "essential" God in one nature, communicating himself to the created world. We see also the importance of Karl Rahner's principle that the "immanent" relationships found within the Trinity between the persons are also operative in the "economic" relationships.

Therefore, as within the Trinity, so in the order of salvation, only the Son and the Holy Spirit proceed from the Father. Hence, only the Son and Holy Spirit can be "sent" into our world. The Son of God is sent by the Father into this world and he alone assumes humanity to reveal or image the invisible Father. The Spirit that binds the Father and Son together in love also proceeds from that love between the Father and the Son. The Spirit, therefore, has a very special function in our regard that flows out of his unique personhood as the bond of love between the Father and the Son. The entire Trinity has equally loved this world and ourselves in this world, yet the Spirit is sent into our hearts to effect our sanctification. He is the one who is always the loving force, always uniting and differentiating in love.

If scripture attests to the fact that this Holy Spirit is given to us and performs certain actions, it must mean that he is "sent" in a most personalized way, befitting his personal way of being within the Trinity. He is "present" to us in a similar way as he is present to the Father and the Son. As the energies of God, operating as one nature, are uncreated and never begin or cease to operate, so in a similar manner, if the "economic" actions of the Holy Spirit are linked with the "immanent" action of the same Spirit, such actions, being divine, do not begin or cease to operate. Being sent by the Father and the Son, the Holy Spirit does not undergo any change or separation from the Father or the Son. The change must be within us who receive him. This is what is called "created grace." It is especially by the created grace called *sanctifying grace* that we are changed and enter into a new relationship with the Trinity by becoming truly a child of God the Father, a brother with Jesus and his Spouse and a temple of the Holy Spirit.

It is imperative that we keep in mind, as "primal grace," the uncreated energies of God which possess within the one nature of the triune God the individuated, personalized relations of the three persons, Father, Son and Holy Spirit, to us. And these personalized relations, like the uncreated energies, do not come and go. They are always present. What comes and goes, what begins, exists and can be destroyed is our response in knowledge and love to that presence of the three persons, operating eternally in accordance with their constitutive personalities. This is the created relationship that flows from the primal grace. Why this distinction is so important is that we must hold from scripture that God truly communicates *himself* to us. His communication is not indirectly through grace, i.e., a created grace, for then we would not truly be receiving God the gift, but we would be receiving a *thing* called sanctifying grace. This is a created relationship that can grow, be given, can be withdrawn as a gift, but it flows intrinsically from *the* gift that is God himself.

Thomas Aquinas well describes God's presence to us in knowledge and love through the created grace called sanctifying grace:

> Over and above the ordinary and common manner in which God is present in all things, namely, by his essence, his power and his presence, as the cause is present in the effects which are a participation in his goodness, there is another and a special presence which is appropriate to rational nature, a presence by which God is said to be present as that which is known is present to the being who knows, and as that which is loved is present to the being who loves. And because a rational and a loving creature by its operation in knowing and loving is placed in contact with God himself, for that reason it is said that God by this special manner of presence is not only *in* a rational creature, but also that he *dwells* in it as in his temple. No other effect than sanctifying grace can be the reason why of this new manner of presence of the Divine Person. It is therefore solely by sanctifying grace that the Divine Person is thus sent forth and proceeds temporarily. . . . And al-

ways, together with grace, one receives also the Holy Spirit himself, who is thus given and sent.[3]

This important text summarizes well for us how God can be present to us through the created relationship called *sanctifying grace*. But there can be a danger in such a presentation. It could appear as though the Holy Spirit comes to us as a result of such a relationship and is not present always in the uncreated energies of love that are operative regardless of our cooperation or even knowledge of them. The Holy Spirit is always operating and is always being sent by the Father and the Son, this even from the beginning of time. But when we open ourselves in a conversion away from sinfulness and selfish love to his loving presence, then there is produced a new relationship that is capable of growth in greater knowledge and love.

The Holy Spirit is constantly being given to all human persons, if they would only open up to his loving presence. The beginning and the growth depend upon our response and cooperation. This relationship (not the Holy Spirit) grows in us every time we open up in ever conscious cooperation with the Spirit. Throughout the day, whenever we cooperate with the actual graces given us to perform virtues, especially that of charity, in seeking to do all for the greater glory of God, this relationship grows in greater intensity. The Holy Spirit takes over our spiritual faculties and unites us more intensely with the Trinity in knowledge of God's loving presence and in love as a response to God's ever-present love.

If we believe that the Holy Spirit comes as a consequence upon sanctifying grace, we tend to objectivize grace as a "thing" and the Holy Spirit would be thus present, not immediately and directly, but in the "thing" called grace. Representative of such "thingafying" grace and the presence of the indwelling Trinity is the following statement, found so often in similar books that deal with God's indwelling presence:

> Scarcely has mortal sin been committed, however, when the Divine Guests depart, saying again and again those fearful words that rang out from the temple of Jerusalem when the day of its ruin had come. "Let us go hence! Let us go hence!" The soul thus

abandoned by God and his angels becomes the den of demons and the haunt of those venomous creatures that are none other than its malignant passions.[4]

A substantial presence

What we find in the scriptural texts concerning the Holy Spirit's relationships with us Christians is solidly confirmed by the early Fathers. They fought heretics, such as the Arians, Macedonians and the *Pneumatomachoi*, who held that the Holy Spirit was not a divine person, but was a created gift of God.

The basic arguments of the Fathers universally centered around Athanasius' reasoning that if the Holy Spirit effects man's participation in the divine nature, the Spirit cannot be a created being, since he brings about an effect, man's divinization, that is above all creatures.

Gregory of Nazianzen rather dramatically, but to the point, phrases the patristic argument that the Holy Spirit truly effects our divinization and does so because he is truly divine.

I cannot believe that I am saved by one who is my equal. If the Holy Spirit is not God, let him first be made God, and then let him deify me his equal.... Why do you grudge me a complete regeneration? Why do you make me, who am a temple of the Holy Spirit as of God, the habitation of a creature?[5]

If the Holy Spirit brings us into the likeness of Jesus Christ so as to become truly God's children, he must be, as the Fathers insist, *substantially* present, i.e., according to his very being as the *Holy Spirit* who by his substance is the Sanctifier. He himself must live in us and communicate to us the divine life. If he merely gives us a created grace, we are not being *gifted* through the Holy Spirit with the triune God's very nature. Sanctifying grace can never exist separated from the Holy Spirit, working in his substantial presence in an analogous manner to his operations within the Trinity.

This point is extremely important. For if the real Spirit of Christ and the Father is touching us with his substantial presence, then we can indeed hope to become completely regenerated, "born of the Spirit" (Jn 3:6). We must avoid any unscriptural and unpatristic view that would hold our justification as children of God to be only an extrinsic title given to us through the blood of Christ, without a genuine regeneration and divinization as taught so universally by all of the early Fathers.

Cyril of Alexandria aptly summarizes this universal teaching among the Fathers:

> It is untrue to say that we cannot be one with God except by union of will. For above that union there is another union more sublime and far superior, which is wrought by the communication of the Divinity to man, who, while keeping his own nature, is, so to speak, transformed into God, just as iron plunged into fire becomes fiery, and while remaining iron seems changed into fire.... Union with God cannot exist otherwise than by participation with the Holy Spirit, diffusing in us the sanctification proper to himself, imprinting and engraving on our souls the divine likeness.[6]

Didymus, the blind man of Alexandria, also insists strongly that God alone is able to communicate himself to us substantially. He argues that such things as arts and sciences, virtues and vices dwell in us as accidental qualities and not as substances. But the indwelling of the Holy Spirit is his substantial self as present and sanctifying.

> Now it is the proper substance of the Holy Spirit who dwells in the just and who sanctifies them and it belongs only to the Three Persons of the Holy Trinity, to be able, by their substance, to penetrate into souls.[7]

Praying in the Spirit

The good news that Jesus came to give us is that the kingdom of God is truly within us. It is the inner, hidden, dwelling presence of the Holy Spirit, given to us in baptism in an embryonic relationship whereby, through the inner operations of the Spirit upon us in faith, hope and love, we become more and more aware that we live a new life in Christ Jesus.

This indwelling Holy Spirit teaches us how to pray deeply in the heart. He leads us beyond our idols constructed about God to live in the mystery of the circular movement of the Father, Son and Spirit's inter-love relationships. He bears witness to our spirit that we are truly children of God. He teaches us a new language of praise and worship, so that prayer is no longer a thing we do before we do something else, but it is a constant attitude of being "toward" God in self-surrendering love to him, the ground of our being. The Spirit leads us into deeper contemplation and more intimate union with the Father through Jesus Christ by purifying the heart through a constant spirit of repentance. He destroys the spirit of the Pharisee in the synagogue and replaces it with that of the repentant publican who in reverence and sorrow cannot even lift his face to God, but strikes his breast and whispers: "God, be merciful to me, a sinner" (Lk 18:14).

The Spirit leads us ever deeper into our heart where an abiding sense of sorrow for sins and fear of ever losing the loving mercy of God create a contrite, humble heart. Broken in the spirit of egoism and independence, we humbly turn in our poverty toward God. Stripped of our own power to heal ourselves, we cry out for healing and the Spirit of love brings it about on the deepest levels of our being, in our "heart."

Because the Spirit is truly communicating within us his personality as the bond of love between the Father and Son, he teaches us to pray in spirit and truth by convincing us through an outpouring of faith, hope and love that we are truly God's children, divinized by grace, made participators of the divine nature (2 P 1:14). The sanctifying Spirit makes us become what Jesus Christ is by nature. He truly divinizes us, regenerating us with God's very own life.

The living Word of God

In prayer the Holy Spirit continually reveals to us the deeper meanings of the Word of God as revealed in holy scripture. It becomes "something alive and active; it cuts like any double-edged sword but more finely: it can slip through the place where the soul is divided from the spirit, or joints from the marrow; it can judge the secret emotions and thoughts. No created thing can hide from him; everything is uncovered and open to the eyes of the one to whom we must give account of ourselves" (Heb 4:12-13).

In such infusion of knowledge and understanding of the Word of God, the Holy Spirit opens to us the treasures of the mysteries of faith. God is alive and in process always of revealing himself through his Son in his Spirit. The Spirit reveals to us all we need to know about the Father and his Son, Jesus Christ. We begin to experience how Christ lives in our hearts through faith and by being built up on love, we "will with all the saints have strength to grasp the breadth and the length, the height and the depth" (Eph 3:18). We will be filled with the utter fullness of God. And that fullness is experienced as flowing within us and, in that oneness with the indwelling divine life, we can easily discover this same "unconcealing" divine life all about us in the surrounding world of human beings and things.

Such Christians cry out constantly for greater release of the Holy Spirit in their hearts. They are seized by him and given to Jesus Christ who, as the way, the truth and the life, leads them to the Father, all together dwelling within them. The riches of the mysteries of God are inexhaustible like an abyss. Yet prayer becomes more an action of yielding to the indwelling Spirit so as to enter into the very movement of triadic life that is present and dynamically exercising its life from within. It is to go beyond images, words and even feelings to reach through the indwelling Spirit a state of complete abandonment to the heavenly Father.

Totally surrendered to God, we live only for him as each moment brings us an occasion to be a living gift back to God as he gives himself to us in his triadic movement of love. A new threshold of union with God has been reached in such prayer of the heart under the guidance of the indwelling Holy Spirit, for we have passed through the dread of the purification of the senses. God has taken away from us all attachment to sense pleasures as we have learned to let go in the darkness of our inner poverty to be guided by the "luminous-dark" presence of the indwelling Trinity. Now no thing or no human person can be the source of any attraction without a conscious submission of that relationship to God's holy will. God is finally, through the presence of the indwelling Spirit, becoming our God!

The work of the indwelling Spirit

As the Spirit is the loving presence between the Father and the Son, he can be present to us only by his works of love. In the Old Testament he is the creative force of God moving into chaos, darkness and death. He draws the "void" into a sharing of God's being (Gn 1:2). He was a transforming power that in the anointing of kings fashioned them into servants to rule God's people. He was the "seeing voice" of the prophets of old who foretold the messianic age.

Human beings were given new hearts by God's Spirit (Ez 36:26). God had prophesied that this living presence of his Spirit among his people would be poured out in a future age in great abundance (Jn 3:1-2). And within us, through the growth of faith, hope and love in prayer, we experience the first great work that the Spirit effects in our lives as he sanctifies and justifies us. Paul describes this transforming power of the Spirit in our hearts:

> These are the sort of people some of you were once, but now you have been washed clean, and sanctified and justified through the name of the Lord Jesus Christ and through the Spirit of our God. (1 Co 6:11)

God, through the Spirit of love, removes our iniquities from us as far as the east is from the west (Ps 103:12). "I it is, I it is, who must blot out everything and not remember your sins" (Is 43:25). The Spirit witnesses in the depths of our hearts that in Christ's death, God condemned sin in the flesh (Rm 8:3). Jesus Christ has passed over from sin and death into a new creation. His new and glorious life living within us makes him the new Adam and Lord of the universe. He is capable in this exalted existence in glory of bestowing upon us this new life that he has received from the Spirit of his Father by revealing to us that we are forgiven our sins and have been established as children of his Father. The indwelling Spirit is God's life-giving "breath" that the risen Jesus is always breathing upon us.

Amidst so much darkness that still lives within us and outside of us, the Spirit reveals to us that God has saved us, "by means of the cleansing water of rebirth and by renewing us with the Holy Spirit which he has so generously poured over us through Jesus Christ our savior" (Tt 3:4-7). This indwelling Spirit of the risen Christ brings us into direct contact with the spiritualized body-person of Jesus risen who dwells also within us along with the heavenly Father who Jesus promised would come with him to abide in us as in a mansion (Jn 14:23).

We are always through the indwelling Spirit caught up in an ongoing process of becoming God's children through the regeneration that the Spirit brings us, allowing us to be "born of the Spirit" (Jn 3:6). The light of the Spirit leads us out of all darkness and illusion. We are gradually enlightened by the light of his indwelling presence to know the truth that we are in Christ, a part of his risen body. That same Spirit, that drove Jesus Christ to "pass over" from his own independence into total surrendering love to the Father on our behalf on the cross, reveals to us that Jesus, the image of the Father's love for us individually, still loves us with that infinity of love. "For me he died," cried Paul in a transforming knowledge given him by the Spirit that dwelt within him (Ga 2:20).

As we yield to such a dynamic love pouring over our consciousness and the deep layers of our unconscious, we experience a new freedom of being children of God, loved so immensely by God himself. Fears and anxieties are shed as we experience new powers to love, to be "toward" God and ourselves and our neighbors. The dried bones from the chaotic past take on new life as the Spirit breathes gently over them. We come out of the past as an old man waking from the dream suddenly to find himself a youth, full of life and exciting hope of what will be.

An expanded consciousness floods my whole being as I feel the body, soul, spirit relationships within me come together in an integrated, whole person. "God, it is good to be alive and healthy!" I realize the divine uncreated energies of God's triadic life flowing through me, in every part, on every level. I am a branch and God is the vine. I breathe in his breath. I am alive with his life. Like a butterfly, with wet, tightly-packed wings, I stretch upward toward the heavenly kingdom. The wings dry, strengthen, lift me aloft to new, dizzying heights of union with God.[8]

Freed from sin by the light of the indwelling Spirit of Jesus risen, we no longer wish to live in darkness. "No one who has been begotten by God sins; because God's seed remains inside him, he cannot sin when he has been begotten by God" (1 Jn 3:9). As the Spirit constantly reveals to us from within our true identity as children, loved infinitely by a perfect Father through Jesus Christ who has died for us, we can live each moment in him and with him. We can learn to accept our true identity that is a becoming unto the full, matured children of God as Jesus was. But this takes place only in the present *now* that is the only *locus*, the meeting-place of God's eternal *now* of his love for us in Christ Jesus. The Holy Spirit progressively brings about our regeneration as children of God to the degree that we yield to his illuminations and inspiration, poured forth from within us. These give us knowledge and the power of love to live according to the revealed knowledge that the Spirit pushes us at each moment to live, namely, that we possess an inner dignity as children of God, one with Christ, a part of his very body.

Augustine, commenting on the words of Psalm 82:6, "You too are gods, sons of the Most High, all of you," expresses well our human dignity as children of God:

> He who justifies is the very same who deifies, because in justifying us he makes us children of God. . . . Now, if we are children of God, by that very fact we are gods, doubtless not by a natural generation, but a grace of adoption. One holy, indeed, is the Son of God by nature, the one only God with the Father, our Lord and Savior Jesus Christ. . . . The others who become gods so become by his grace; they are not born of his substance so as to become what he is, but they attain to a divine sonship by the favor of his generosity, in order that they may be made co-heirs of Christ.[9]

We are, according to Paul, alive by the Spirit, so we must walk always by the Spirit. "If you are guided by the Spirit you will be in no danger of yielding to self-indulgence . . . the Spirit is totally against such a thing. . . . If you are led by the Spirit, no law can touch you" (Ga 5:16-18).

Fruit of the Spirit

The presence of the Holy Spirit within us is not a delectation to be enjoyed without any reference to daily living and growth into greater life as children of God. The indwelling Spirit prods us to greater complexity, to greater pruning and inner discipline. For with Paul, we all continually realize that we are caught within the dialectic of two forces: the power of darkness and evil and that of the Spirit of Jesus which is holiness and light. We are to live according to the Spirit of Jesus. This Spirit creates the new life of Christ within us. He also fosters and brings it to its fullness in the proportion that the Spirit becomes normative in guiding the Christians to make choices according to the mind of Christ. Ideally the life of a Christian is freed from any extrinsic legalism and is guided by that interior communication that he receives when he turns within and listens to the Spirit of Jesus.

By the Spirit produced, we Christians have no doubt as to which spirit is guiding us—the spirit of the world or the Spirit of the risen Jesus. Paul described these two opposite sets of fruit. He ends up describing the authentic fruit of the Holy Spirit:

What the Spirit brings is very different: love, joy, peace, patience, kindness, goodness, trustfulness, gentleness and self-control. There can be no law against these things like that, of course. You cannot belong to Christ Jesus unless you crucify all self-indulgent passions and desires. Since the Spirit is our life, let us be directed by the Spirit. (Ga 5:22-25)

It is through the Spirit that God who is love is able to communicate to us the power to be loving, filled with joy, abounding in patience and, in general, putting on the mind of Christ in all thoughts, words and deeds. The work of the Spirit that dwells within us is to pour out the love of God into our hearts since he is given to us (Rm 5:5). The outpouring of the Spirit is the filling up in our hearts of the love of God. What is impossible to us who still carry sin in our members (Rm 7:23) becomes possible by the indwelling Spirit. We are able to love at each moment with the very love of God that abides within us. "Anyone who lives in love lives in God, and God lives in him" (1 Jn 4:16). The love of God through the Spirit gradually possesses our heart. It is the same love with which God the Father loves his Son and ourselves as his children. We are to yield to this inner power and live in it in all our human relationships. The Holy Spirit dwelling within us is the love of God abiding in us and empowering us to become loving human beings. It is in the power of the Holy Spirit that we can be loving.

To attain this union of active love with Jesus Christ, the Spirit of Jesus reveals to us how we are to do always all actions to please God, to lead "a life acceptable to him in all its aspects" (Col 1:10). But this cannot be done unless we are ready to put to death our carnal desires and put on the mind of Christ. It is the Spirit that helps us. "The Spirit too comes to help us in our weakness" (Rm 8:26). The Spirit prays by allowing us to be present to the Father's overwhelming love for us. But above all, the Spirit pours out this divine love into our hearts. It is by the Spirit's love infused into us that we can die to selfishness and live to Christ. Through the love of God poured into our hearts we can be always patient and kind, never jealous or boastful or conceited or rude or selfish. We need no more to take offense or be resentful. We will always be ready to excuse, to trust, to hope and to endure whatever comes. For love is the greatest gift of God. It is truly the Holy Spirit himself operating freely within us (1 Co 13:4-13).

Sent to build community

The Holy Spirit brings us into a deep union with Jesus Christ so that his name is always on our lips and in our hearts. Our life becomes a *oneness* in him as we seek to live each moment in the transcendence of the risen Jesus. This is the work of the Spirit:

> And we, with our unveiled faces reflecting like mirrors the brightness of the Lord, all grow brighter and brighter as we are turned into the image that we reflect; this is the work of the Lord who is Spirit. (2 Co 3:18)

Through the experience that is always ongoing of being one in Christ, living members of his very body, the Spirit prompts us outward, not only to discover Christ in others, but to labor incessantly to bring Jesus forth in their lives. The Spirit is the builder of the body of Christ. "There is one Body, one Spirit, just as you were all called into one and the same hope when you are called" (Eph 4:4).

We see that in the life of Jesus, whenever the Spirit is associated with him, it is in the light of his mission. His mission was to fight against the world and its sinfulness and to conquer it. When Jesus preached in the synagogue in Nazareth, he read from Isaiah 61:1-2:

> He has sent me to bring the good news to the poor,
> to proclaim liberty to captives
> and to the blind new sight,
> to set the downtrodden free,
> to proclaim the Lord's year of favor. (Lk 4:18)

This was his mission and he was anointed in his baptism by John the Baptist for this work of setting us free. The Spirit anointed him to preach, to heal and perform miracles. And he pours out his Spirit upon his followers that they might also be anointed by the Spirit for a sharing in the mission of Jesus.

> "As the Father sent me,
> so am I sending you."
> After saying this he breathed on them and said:
> "Receive the Holy Spirit.
> For those whose sins you forgive,
> they are forgiven;
> for those whose sins you retain,
> they are retained." (Jn 20:21-23)

Ambassadors for Christ

The Spirit is poured into our hearts, not only that we might rejoice in the good news that we are God's children, but that we might go out and bring the good news that all human beings are called by God to become through the Spirit of love also God's children. Jesus is to extend his anointed work through his Spirit poured out into his members in order to take away sins, liberate mankind from all effects of sins and to bring about a new creation that will be the reconciliation of the entire world to the Father in fulfillment of his eternal plan in creating all things in and through his word. "It was God who reconciled us to himself through Christ and gave us the work of handing on this reconciliation. . . . So we are ambassadors for Christ; it is as though God were appealing through us, and the appeal that we make in Christ's name is: Be reconciled to God" (2 Co 5:18-20).

Paul writes to the Corinthian church that the various members have been given diverse gifts by the Spirit, all to build up the body of Christ:

> There is a variety of gifts but always the same Spirit; there are all sorts of services to be done, but always to the same Lord; working in all sorts of different ways in different people, it is the same God who is working in all of them. The particular way in which the Spirit is given to each person is for a good purpose. . . . All these are the work of one and the same Spirit, who distributes different gifts to different people just as he chooses. (1 Co 12:4-11)

Paul gives here a list of nine gifts or charisms that serve to build up an individual, praying community. In Romans 12:6-8 he gives another, broader list of charisms, but all are to build up the one body, the Church, whose head is Christ and whose members are Christians in whom dwells the Holy Spirit. The Spirit gives all of us charisms for the good of the whole body, the Church. In Ephesians 4:11-13, Paul gives still another list along the lines of hierarchical functions.

But what the indwelling Spirit within us reveals is that our proper dignity as children of God consists in our functioning within the body of Christ out of love to serve the whole community. The sign of true Christian maturity into the "new man" (Eph 2:5; 4:24) is our readiness to put aside our egoism and live for the good of the whole. It is according to the degree of conscious, corporate unity with Christ, the head, and all of the members that each individual grows in perfection and can assist in building up the whole body. "If we live by the truth and in love, we shall grow in all ways into Christ, who is the head" (Eph 4:15).

The fruit that we are called to bring forth within the body of Christ is love for each other, which again, as we have seen, is the principal fruit of the indwelling Spirit. We know that Jesus Christ lives in each of us as is shown in the love that we show toward all others. This is possible only through the work of the Spirit within us. It is this truth that we have comprehended by the help of the Spirit of the indwelling Jesus who sets us free (Jn 8:32).

Power of the Holy Spirit

Jesus had promised that he would ask the Father to send the Spirit of truth upon his followers (Jn 14:15-29) to be with them, in the Church, in each Christian, and to stay with them forever. This Spirit is meant not merely to abide within us believers, but to send us forth in love as he is being sent forth in love by the Father and the Son. The Spirit would teach the followers of Jesus everything and would bring to their consciousness everything that Jesus had said and done (Jn 14:25-27).

The Spirit would teach Christians about Jesus and would empower them to become witnesses of Jesus, just as the Spirit witnesses to him (Jn 15:26). This same Spirit will unfold, reveal the plan of salvation to the believers in Jesus and give them true judgment according to Christ's plan. The world's sin is disbelief in Jesus. The Spirit will expose that and will lead the followers of Jesus into the complete truth (Jn 16:7-15).

Jesus had to leave his disciples in order to be freed from space and time to exist in a new form. After his resurrection he would be able to abide within his followers along with his Father and his Spirit (Jn 14:23). He would give them a new baptism with the Holy Spirit (Ac 1:5), and the great promise that Jesus continues to make to all of us modern Christians as he made it to his apostles: "You will receive power when the Holy Spirit comes on you, and then you will be my witnesses not only in Jerusalem but throughout Judaea and Samaria, and indeed to the ends of the earth" (Ac 1:8).

After Pentecost when they had received the outpouring of the Holy Spirit, the first Christian community in Jerusalem witnessed to what, like the apostles, we also could receive: filled with the Spirit, they went forth to witness to the inner transformation that took place through their baptism by Jesus in the Holy Spirit. They preached and witnessed fearlessly to the risen Jesus. They performed signs and miracles. Peter confesses to the astonished Jews: "What you see and hear is the outpouring of that Spirit" (Ac 2:33).

As we read the Acts of the Apostles and the epistles of Paul, we see the power of the Spirit that came upon the followers of Jesus. They pray for courage and power to preach the message, to heal and work miracles through the name of Jesus and they received that power (Ac 4:29-31). The early community remained faithful to the teaching of the apostles, to the brotherhood, to the breaking of bread and to prayers. They shared everything in common and worked miracles and signs and God blessed their community with new members (Ac 2:42-47).

If problems arose, they consulted the Spirit within them and within the *koinonia* or Christian community. "It has been decided by the Holy Spirit and by ourselves . . ." (Ac 15:28). They seek the mind of God through the Spirit's guidance in prayer and fasting (Ac 13:2). "We and the Holy Spirit" (Ac 5:32) becomes the continued experience within that early Church, the fruit of Jesus sending upon those who believe in him the Holy Spirit. Stephen and Philip, deacons, are filled with the Spirit and preach and work miracles with great power. Converts from among not only Jews but also the Gentiles are brought into the Church by the Holy Spirit being given to them when they are prayed over by the elders.

Confronting the world with the Spirit

Jesus sends us the Spirit in order that sin, the result of the world's darkness in us, be eradicated from us. But the Spirit within us drives us out into the world to confront the chaos, darkness and death that exist there. The life in the spirit is to be a life of struggle and fight against sin in whatever form it appears, in our own personal lives or in those of others or in the society in which we live. The world cannot accept the Spirit since it neither sees nor recognizes him (Jn 14:17). There is an aggressive hostility on the part of the world against the Spirit and the work of Christ to restore unity in the human race. The world will hate the disciples of Christ and persecute them (Jn 15:18-20).

But the Christians in the Spirit are not to run away from the world, but are to be the "ambassadors of Christ," bearing the Word of God. The Spirit dwells within us (Jn 14:17) and we are to be Christ's witnesses to his values of the gospel by our lives lived in love and unity. We are to be led by the Spirit of love. To refuse to be led by this Spirit is sin. Even when persons unknowingly operate out of transcendent, self-forgetting love, they are being guided by the Spirit. To sin is to assert self over the Spirit of love that lives for loving service toward the others.

The Spirit of love, God's love, has been operating in the Old Testament times, but also among all persons of good will outside the Old and New Covenants. God has poured his Spirit of love into the hearts of all who willingly submit to live for the absolute God in loving service to their neighbors. This Spirit of love operates in the most simple things of life: in the act of giving a cup of cold water to a traveler, a letter written to a loved one, visiting the lonely and sickly. His unifying force is felt in all technological and medical advances brought about by human beings cooperating with the uncreated energies of God's love, found in every facet of human living.

This Spirit of the risen Christ is operating in the lives of a man and woman deeply in love who experience this divine, unifying force of love in their conjugal union as they leave selfish *eros* to find their own beings and to expand by giving without reserve to the other to bring forth in that overflowing energy of life a new life, made to the image and likeness of God himself. This is creativity at its highest, union through *agape,* the truest sign of the presence of the Spirit.

This Spirit is working as a mother and father work patiently to form their child, as religious or lay persons teach students, as professional workers, skilled and unskilled men and women, do their daily work with loving dedication to serve others. Such persons in their very work experience a true liberation, an expansion of their inner being, a resurrection to a new and higher level of life in the Spirit of Jesus Christ. This may be consciously in the performance of our "secular" actions. Yet the law of the Spirit holds true in all cases: to "ascend" to a higher form of existence, a greater liberation, a new level of oneness in love with others with a new consciousness of our own individuated personhood, we must undergo a "descending" process. This is a dying to the elements in our total make-up that act as obstacles to the operations of the indwelling Spirit.

In all details of our lives the Spirit of God is operating to effect the one desire of God in our regard: "What God wants is for you all to be holy" (1 Th 4:3). For this purpose God . . . "gives you his Holy Spirit" (1 Th 4:8). There is no area of our lives that is not touched at every moment by the Spirit of the risen Jesus. No area of our lives lies in the strictly "profane," which means, that all things belong to God's Spirit of love. The Spirit of God fills the whole world. He holds all things together (Heb 1:3; Col 1:17). He is present to all human beings, communicating God's great love for them and drawing them into a greater image-likeness to his Son, Jesus Christ.

> The Spirit of the Lord, indeed, fills the whole world, and that which holds all things together knows every word that is said. The man who gives voice to injustice will never go unnoticed, nor shall avenging Justice pass him by. (Wi 1:7-8)

Peter De Rosa well describes the working of the Spirit among those who serve others in love, whether they do it knowingly or unknowingly in the Spirit of love:

> Whoever rights wrongs, feeds the hungry, cares for the dispossessed not merely with enthusiasm but with dogged determination, whoever is meek and poor of heart; whoever is sensitive toward the numerous little heartaches people suffer, is—knowingly or unknowingly—an envoy of Christ. And whoever shares in Christ's mission, shares in the Fire of the Spirit.[10]

Be filled with the Spirit

Paul gives this as a command to those who are followers of Christ by choice and God's grace. "Be filled with the Spirit" (Eph 5:18). This is the end of our lives. Each moment of each day we must desire to be baptized by Jesus Christ in his Holy Spirit.

Each time we choose to surrender ourselves to the inner guidance, the Spirit assuredly gives us an infusion of faith, hope and love. When such surrendering becomes habitual, we can call it *infused contemplation,* the gift of the Holy Spirit whereby he gives to our spiritual faculties of understanding and willing, of knowing and loving, an habitual experience of the transcendent God, Father, Son and Spirit, immanently present within us and drawing us into a union of his triadic family. In this prayerful, adoring communion an intense union of wills takes place. We feel *one* with the Trinity. The three persons, Father, Son and Spirit, are constantly present to us and we to them in loving surrender.

Yet along with the heightened sense of oneness with God, the Spirit gives us a new understanding of our *uniqueness*. We know our identity in God's Spirit of love. In saying *I* to the *thou* of God, we know in a new awareness how individually and beautifully we are loved by God. "I have called thee by thy name. Thou art mine" (Is 43:1). We experience the loving gaze of the heavenly Father, imaged by the presence of Jesus Christ his only-begotten Son who is always giving himself unto the last drop of blood on the cross. In their look of love we spring into *new* being. The Trinity's personalized love, experienced now more deeply and more totally (less conceptually), calls us to be the unique person God wishes us to be.

We can afford to give our life away and truly find it in our gift of love to another. We step out into life's fast-moving stream and eagerly embrace each moment as a *now* moment of growing in greater love for God and neighbor. Each person, thing, event encountered becomes an *epiphany,* a manifestation of God appearing in our lives in a new incarnational form. As the Spirit was present, hovering over Mary in the incarnation, so the same Spirit hovers over each moment to "unconceal" for us through faith, hope and love the loving, incarnational presence of Jesus Christ who leads us to the Father.

Nothing surprises us or upsets us, because the Spirit's quickening of faith, hope and love allows us to see "inside" of all things and there to discover God's loving action. We see that all things really work unto good to those who love the Lord (Rm 8:28). Praise comes to our lips readily as we see God in a diaphany, a shining through each happening of each moment.

To live in such a mystical union with the Trinity is impossible by our own power. But it is the Spirit that teaches us how to pray as we ought (Rm 8:26-27). It should not be considered an extraordinary state of prayer for anyone who sincerely wishes to be continually baptized by

Jesus Christ in his Spirit. We can all receive the gift of contemplation that is a process of continued growth in loving submission to Jesus Christ as Lord. But this is impossible without the Spirit (1 Co 12:3). God wishes us all to grow in mystical union with the Trinity.

We are all called by Jesus Christ in his Spirit to enter into a consciousness of communing with the Holy Trinity that knows no interruption. For such who grow in the baptism in the Holy Spirit, this admits of a continued increase in awareness of the immanence of the indwelling Trinity within them. As they yield themselves in each moment to the uncreated energies of God divinizing them into children of God, they become more vitally aware through the indwelling Spirit that they are loved as children by an infinitely loving Father.

The true test of what degree of contemplation we have reached is tested by the life we live. If we are aware of the indwelling Spirit who leads us to a living knowledge and love of the Father and Jesus Christ, then we are truly made by that Spirit's power into new creatures in Christ Jesus (2 Co 5:17). This new state of being in Christ will show itself consistently in our lives through the love we have toward one another and by the humility we manifest in authentic service to meet their needs. True mysticism of the indwelling Trinity and true baptism in the Holy Spirit will always be measured by the degree that we allow the Spirit to transfigure us into love which must then go out into a loving service toward others. True love of God will always be a true love for other human beings. Ultimately there can be only one love and that is the Spirit of the Trinity bringing forth within us the relationship that we can call "graced-love." The truly charismatic Christian, baptized in the Spirit continuously in the circumstances of his daily life, is a mystic who has been transformed into a living incarnation of God's love for mankind.[11]

> Let us love one another since love comes from God
> And everyone who loves is begotten by God and knows God.
> Anyone who fails to love can never have known God.
> As long as we love one another God will live in us
> And his love will be complete in us . . .
> God is love and anyone who lives in love lives in God
> And God lives in him. (1 Jn 4:7-16)

Notes

1. Athanasius, *Contra Gentes* 41 (*Select Works and Letters,* in *LNPF,* 4:26).
2. This text, as George T. Montague, S.J. points out as the common consensus of modern scriptural exegetes, "refers here not to the individual body of the Christian but to the Christian community as such," in *The Holy Spirit: Growth of a Biblical Tradition* (New York: Paulist Press, 1976), 13.
3. Thomas Aquinas, *Summa Theologica,* p. 151, no. 3: 1, Q. XLIII.
4. B. Forget, O.P., *The Indwelling of the Holy Spirit in the Souls of the Just* (New York: Paulist Press, 1921), 130.
5. Gregory of Nazianzen, *Oratio* 34.12 (*LNPF,* 337).
6. Cyril of Alexandria, *Commentary on the Gospel of St. John* (*PG* 74.293).
7. Didymus the Blind, *De Spiritu Sancto* 25 (*PG* 39.1055-56).
8. G. A. Maloney, S.J., *Inward Stillness* (Denville: Dimension Books, 1976), 64.
9. Augustine, *In Psalmo 49,* n. 2 (*PL* 86.565).
10. Peter De Rosa, *Come, Holy Spirit* (Milwaukee: Bruce Co., 1968), 60.
11. Much of this present chapter has already been published in my work that is now out of print, *Invaded by God* (Denville: Dimension Books, 1979). But since this work is not available to most readers, I wish to make this chapter available to them by incorporating those ideas that first appeared in that work.

Chapter 9

Eucharist and the Holy Trinity

The Holy Trinity and the eucharist

Have you ever noticed what a difference takes place in your relationships with friends when they invite you to eat a meal at their table? They buy food and carefully prepare it. Possibly they serve you a good table wine to warm your heart. As they offer you food and drink, they are saying symbolically. "By this food and drink we offer you our love. We want to nourish new life in you by sharing ourselves with you, our love, our presence in your life."

In no physical sense are they, or their love for you, the food and drink; nor are they in any way literally inside the nourishment they offer you. And yet in their loving self-giving they become present to you in the "breaking of the bread." The food and drink are symbol-carriers making it possible to "act out" in a physical, visible action a *ritual,* a hidden, mysterious spiritual reality we call *love.* Human interiority is not only expressed through such actions, but the inside feelings and movements become a transforming power far beyond what was locked up inside the human heart.

God's loving gift

The eucharist is the place in our human space and time where, in a similar "meal," God reaches, as it were, the peak of his inner trinitarian love. The tremendous mutual self-giving of Father and Son and Spirit of love cannot contain itself. It wants to burst forth, to be shared with others. God gives himself to us created beings in his many gifts.

Theologians speak of the many modes or ways in which God is present in his creation toward us in communication and communion. We must not objectivize God's presence, God's giving of himself to us in the eucharist, as just another of the many ways of being present to us. The eucharist is the center of all other presences of God toward us. In the eucharist, we touch the basis of all reality, the Holy Trinity; here are concentrated the uncreated, personalized, loving energies of God as loving community. God's fullness of love moves toward us in order to transform us into his loving children.

Jesus can so easily be considered as objectively present over there, in "this" host or in "that" tabernacle, and thus we miss the full impact of the mysterious presence of Christ, as the symbol of the trinitarian self-giving in total self-emptying. All other presences of Jesus in our material world meet in the eucharist and are transcended and superseded by this unique presence. It is the climax of God's self-giving to us and, therefore, contains all other forms of his presence "toward" us.

In the eucharist, God literally gives us a part of his very being as we receive the body and blood of Jesus Christ. Cyril of Alexandria wrote, "Fundamentally the eucharist is a victory—a victory of one who is absent to become present in a world which conceals him." Now we have the means whereby we can enter into the fullness of God's intimate sharing of his very own life with us, through touching the glorified, risen humanity of Christ in the eucharist. Not only is it the entire, historical Jesus of Nazareth whom we receive, with all his earthly life of teaching, preaching, healing and miracles, the greatest of which is his passion and death on our behalf, but we receive the risen Lord of glory with the presence of the blessed Trinity.

The Last Supper

As we prayerfully consider the action of Jesus serving the Passover meal on the eve of his passion and death, we discover new insights and applications for our own participation in the eucharist. Jesus used bread and wine, not only symbols of nourishment unto life, but from scripture these were signs of joy and super-abundance for God's chosen people in his promised land.

At the Last Supper, when Jesus first gave himself to his Church-community as eucharist, he gave a blessing. A blessing (in Hebrew, *berakah*) in the Old Testament was a creative act. God blesses his creation, all living creatures, above all human beings, and empowers them to be a similar creative blessing for all creatures given to them by God. God blesses Noah after the flood, and also Abraham, and restores his covenant with the human race through those blessings.

Monika Hellwig describes the importance of a Jewish blessing:

> A blessing is a creative act; it brings something new into existence. It gives an increase of life and of the inheritance that God has bestowed upon his creatures. But a blessing is always expected to make the one who receives it the source of blessing for others; it is not expected to come to rest in its recipient and to end there.[1]

At the Last Supper, Jesus prays at least parts of the great eighteen Tefillah blessings which made up the *berakoth* blessings of the Synagogue service and that of Jewish meals. We catch something of his blessings in John's record of the priestly prayer of Christ (Jn 17:1-26). He glorifies the Father. He offers to him thanksgiving and a prayer of praise and confession that directs all things to the Father as beginning and end, the source of all blessings. Centered upon his heavenly Father, Jesus gives his blessing to his disciples.

It is here that we enter into the peak of God's uncreated energies of love as imaged by Jesus for his followers. John the Evangelist prefaces the love action (eucharist) of Jesus on behalf of his disciples by these words:

> . . . and Jesus knew that the hour had come for him to pass from this world to the Father. He had always loved those who were his in the world, but now he showed how perfect his love was (Jn 13:1).

His hour of the Passover was approaching when Jesus would freely give himself back to the Father in obedience unto death for our sake, so that we, partaking of the Lamb of God, as our food and drink, might be transformed by the gift of himself for us. In the symbolic form of bread and wine Jesus surrenders himself completely to his Father out of love for his followers, including us and all believers down through the centuries. The bread and wine are his flesh and blood to be consumed by his loved ones. He seals his gift by the words, "Do this as a memorial of me" (Lk 22:19). His prayer is an effective prayer but not one that merely asks his followers to return psychologically to the Last Supper and merely remember his great love. It is a prayer of perpetual effectiveness because Jesus is pledging his fidelity to be present as loving sacrifice whenever this ritual is enacted.

Recapitulation through Jesus Christ

We have seen in previous chapters how God's essence as love seeks always to share itself with others. His divine plan was that we would communicate his word by assuming flesh. Into Jesus Christ, fully God and fully man, the Trinity, source of all reality, pours itself. God channels all of his life through him "because God wanted all perfection to be found in him and all things to be reconciled through him and for him" (Col 1:19). Paul tells us: "In his body lives the fullness of divinity and in him you too find your own fulfillment" (Col 2:9).

Jesus is the reconciler of all things in the heavens and on the earth. He will restore the world's lost unity as he draws men and women by the loving attraction of his Spirit into his very body. He at the time of his death and resurrection, in microcosm as it were, re-established or reconciled humanity in himself by destroying sin, death and the distorted element in the flesh. The Trinity exalted him in glory (Ph 2:9-11), making him the "first born among many brethren" (Rm 8:29). At the end of time he will also re-establish all things, raising up the flesh of all mankind by spiritualizing it. He will bring all things completely under his dominion by bestowing the fullness of his divine life upon us for all eternity.

But this re-establishing of divine life in the individual human being is a process that has already begun through baptism and the increase of the Spirit's gifts of faith, hope and love. As we human beings surrender our lives to Jesus Christ, we find in him the center of unity, harmony and meaningfulness which gives to us and the entire world its sense and its value. This is true reality. Jesus becomes the meeting point of God and his creation. The infinite, burning love of God's goodness meets in him and ignites that love in our hearts. We are to ignite love, then, in the hearts of all we meet.

This meeting of the triune life in Christ begins in baptism. "All baptized in Christ, you have all clothed yourselves in Christ" (Ga 3:27). We share in his fullness (Jn 1:16). This divine life grows into ever increasing perfection through the other sacraments, especially confirmation. "In the one Spirit we were all baptized . . . and one Spirit was given to us all to drink" (1 Co 12:13).

The gift of the eucharist

Our centering in Christ and our entrance into the fullness of the trinitarian life reach their peak of perfection in the eucharist. In the eucharist we open ourselves to the ultimate presence of the uncreated energies of God along with the personalized acts of the three persons. It is Christ's resurrected body that comes to us in holy communion. But through this "way," we are led into the holy presence of the Trinity. Now Jesus Christ, the eternal Word of God, the Second Person of the Trinity, can never be separated from his divinized humanity. It is the whole Jesus Christ that comes to us and this glorified God-man can never be separated from the Father and the Holy Spirit relationships.

Gregory of Nyssa compares Jesus in the eucharist to a leaven that "assimilates to itself the whole lump, so in like manner that body to which immortality has been given by God, when it is in ours, translates and transmutes the whole into itself."[2] He argues that Christ, through his eucharistic body, can vivify the whole of mankind just as the same divine power changed the physical bread that Jesus Christ ate into the body of God. Instead of the consumed food becoming part of the person eating it, the eater is transformed into the divine nourishment.[3]

In the incarnation God so loved the world as to give us his only-begotten Son (Jn 3:16). Out of this mystery of his infinite love for us flows the eucharist. As the gift of the eucharist is possible only because of the gift of the God-man, the Logos-made-flesh in the incarnation, so the mystery of the incarnation leads us ultimately to the mystery of the blessed Trinity. Who sees the Son sees also the Father (Jn 14:9). Who receives the body and blood of the Son of God receives not only the Son, but also the Father in his Spirit of love. Who abides in the Son abides in the Father who comes with the Son and his Spirit to dwell within the recipient of the eucharist (Jn 14:23).

Interrelationship between Trinity and eucharist

Thus all three mysteries of the eucharist, the incarnation and the Trinity are intimately connected and explain each other. The mysteries of the Trinity and the incarnation are rooted in God's essence as Love. As the Trinity seeks to share its very own intimate, "family" life with others, the Word leaps forth from out of the heart of the Father. "For when peaceful stillness compassed everything and the night in its swift course was half spent, your all-powerful word from heaven's royal throne bounded, a fierce warrior into the doomed land" (Wi 18:14-15).

God's Word inserts himself into our material world, taking upon himself the form of a servant (Ph 2:8), like to us in all things save sin (Heb 4:15). Not only does God wed himself to the entire, material universe by assuming matter into the trinitarian family, but God also touches each human being. Through the incarnation all human beings are made one through the humanity of Jesus Christ. He is the *new Adam,* the true Father of the human race. We are destined to live with him and through him the very life that was that of God's only-begotten Son.

The eucharist brings this oneness with Christ to fulfillment. Our relationship to the Trinity is not one of an extrinsic adoption, analogous to the true, natural sonship of Jesus Christ. In giving us in the eucharist his very body and blood as food and drink, Jesus Christ wishes to share his very own life with us.

> As I, who am sent by the living Father,
> myself draw life from the Father,
> so whoever eats me will draw life from me.
> This is the bread come down from heaven;

not like the bread our ancestors ate:
they are dead,
but anyone who eats this bread will live for ever. (Jn 6:57-58)

The Father has the fullness of life and he has communicated it to his Son. Jesus Christ, the image of the Father in human form, pours his very own life into all of us who wish to partake of his flesh and blood. He is the "living bread," the bread of life that comes down from heaven. In the incarnation he took upon himself our human flesh. In the eucharist we become assimilated into his human-divine nature.

It is staggering to our weak human minds and impossible to comprehend adequately the depths of God the Father's love for us as imaged in his only-begotten Son. It is *in fact* that we become one with God's only Son. We are *engrafted* into his very being as a branch is inserted into the mainstream of the vine and becomes one total being (Jn 15:1-6).

John Chrysostom perceives this amazing mystery and accentuates the fact of our oneness in the eucharist with Jesus Christ:

> Therefore in order that we may become of his Body, not in desire only, but also in very fact, let us become commingled with that Body. This, in truth, takes place by means of the food which he has given us as a gift, because he desired to prove the love which he has for us. It is for this reason that he has shared himself with us and has brought his Body down to our level, namely, that we might be one with him as the body is joined with the head. And to show the love he has for us he has made it possible for those who desire, not merely to look upon him, but even to touch him and to consume him and to fix their teeth in his Flesh and to be commingled with him; in short, to fulfill all their love. Let us then, come back from that table like lions breathing out fire, thus becoming terrifying to the Devil and remaining mindful of our Head and of the love which he has shown us.[4]

Incorporation into Christ

The Greek Fathers had grasped this union with Christ in the eucharist to be a literal union, a true incorporation into Christ's very own substance. This doctrine they saw as nothing but a commentary on the Pauline and Johannine theology of union with Christ through baptism and eucharist. It was Paul who especially developed the doctrine of the incorporation into Christ's own life. As the apostle to the Gentiles, he boldly developed this key teaching that made Christianity essentially different from paganism. Through the cross Christ destroyed eschatological death and sin. By his own resurrectional life Christ brought us this "new life." "When he died, he died, once for all, to sin, so his life now is life with God; and in that way, you too must consider yourselves to be dead to sin but alive for God in Christ Jesus" (Rm 6:10-11).

But for us to become "alive to God in Christ Jesus," we must be united with Christ; we must be *in Christ*. Paul uses this phrase *in Christ* 164 times and he usually means by this a very real, intimate union with Christ. Baptism puts us into direct contact with the resurrected, glorified Christ, who now, by his spiritualized body-person, can come and truly dwell within us, especially through the eucharist.

> The blessing-cup that we bless is a communion with the blood of Christ, and the bread that we break is a communion with the body of Christ. The fact that there is only one loaf means that, though there are many of us, we form a single body because we all have a share in this one loaf. (1 Co 10:16-17)

We share in the eucharist in Christ's own life, that life of the historical person, Jesus Christ, now gloriously resurrected. We are personally incorporated into Christ, without losing our own identity. Christ lives in us, but we must always be further formed in him (Ga 4:19). By yielding to the life-giving influence of Christ, we Christians are gradually transformed into the image of Christ. This is the only plan and destiny of God, namely, that we are to be transformed into the image of the only-begotten Son, Jesus Christ. "They are the ones he chose specially long ago and intended to become true images of his Son, so that his Son might be the eldest of many brothers. He called those he intended for this, those he called he justified, and with those he justified he shared his glory" (Rm 8:29-30).

In the eucharist Jesus Christ comes to us with the fullness of his divine and human natures. He opens to us "the unsearchable riches of Christ" (Eph 3:8). He loves us in the oneness of the infinite, uncreated energies of love of the Trinity. We join our hearts to that of the God-man and praise and worship the heavenly Father with a perfect love and complete self-surrender.

Union with the Trinity

In our oneness with Jesus Christ in the eucharist we are brought into the heart of the Trinity. Here is the climax of God's eternal plan when he "chose us in Christ, to be holy and spotless, and to live through love in his presence" (Eph 1:4). Sin destroys that likeness to Jesus Christ within us. Our own sinfulness, added to the effects of original sin, hinders the Holy Spirit from raising us to an awareness in grace that Jesus truly lives in us and we in him. But the eucharist (and here we see the need of preparation to receive worthily this sacrament, for repentance and an authentic *metanoia* or conversion) restores and powerfully builds up this oneness with Christ.

Along with an intensification of our own *I-thou* relationship with Jesus Christ, the Holy Spirit brings us into a new awareness of our being also one with the Father and his Holy Spirit. This is the essence of the Last Supper Discourse of Jesus as recorded in John's gospel.

I pray not only for these,
but for those also
who through their words will believe in me.
May they all be one,
Father, may they be one in us,
as you are in me and I am in you,
so that the world may believe it was you who sent me.
I have given them the glory you gave to me,

that they may be one as we are one.
With me in them and you in me,
may they be so completely one
that the world will realize that it was you who sent me
and that I have loved them as much as you loved me. (Jn 17:20-23)

The glory that the Father gave to Jesus was to raise through the incarnation his human nature into a oneness with his "natural" state of being the only-begotten Son of the Father from all eternity. That same glory in the eucharist Jesus is sharing with us to be by the power of the Holy Spirit one with his sonship. We are raised to a supernatural relationship to the blessed Trinity. We become by the fruit of the eucharist, as the Byzantine liturgy of John Chrysostom puts it, "through the fellowship of the Holy Spirit," true participators of God's very own nature (2 P 1:4).

Cyril of Alexandria clearly grasped, not only our divinization as children of God through the eucharist, but also our own union with the Trinity.[5]

> Accordingly we are all one in the Father and in the Son and in the Holy Spirit; one, I say, in unity of relationship of love and concord with God and one another . . . one by conformity in godliness, by communion in the sacred body of Christ, and by fellowship in the one and Holy Spirit and this is a real, physical union.[6]

For if we receive, as we truly believe, the total Jesus Christ, true God and true man, we also receive the Father and his Spirit. For the Son cannot be separated from the glorious union he enjoys with the Father. This is more than a moral union. The Son has received everything that he is from the Father. Unlike an earthly father who sires a child, the heavenly Father is continuously pouring the fullness of his being into his Son. Jesus clearly taught "that I am in the Father and the Father is in me" (Jn 14:10). More clearly yet, Jesus said: "He who sent me is with me, and has not left me to myself" (Jn 8:29).

If Jesus and the Father abide in each other and have come to abide within us in the eucharist (Jn 14:23), the Holy Spirit, as the bond of unity that brings them together and who proceeds as love from their abiding union, also comes and dwells in us. How fittingly are Paul's words applied to our reception of the eucharist: "Your body, you know, is the temple of the Holy Spirit, who is in you since you received him from God" (1 Co 6:19). Again Paul describes the indwelling Spirit as accompanying the love of God in our hearts: "The love of God has been poured into our hearts by the Holy Spirit which has been given us" (Rm 5:5).

Just as the Holy Spirit was present in the incarnation, effecting a begetting by the Father of his Son in human form (Lk 1:35), so the Holy Spirit is present in two ways in the eucharist. The first way is highlighted in most of the Eastern liturgies and is called the *epiklesis.* This literally means a "calling down" of the Holy Spirit to bless and transform the gifts of bread and wine into the body and blood of Jesus Christ. "Send down your Holy Spirit upon us and upon these gifts lying before us . . . and make this bread the precious Body of your Christ, Amen. And that which is in this chalice the precious Blood of your Christ, Amen. Having changed them by your Holy Spirit, Amen, Amen, Amen."[7]

The second presence of the Holy Spirit is the bond of unity between the Father and the Son and all who receive Jesus Christ. This is called the *koinonia* or *fellowship* or communion of the Holy Spirit. This fruit of the eucharist, prayed for in the Eastern liturgies, is mentioned by Paul: "The grace of the Lord Jesus Christ, the love of God and the fellowship of the Holy Spirit be with you all" (2 Co 13:13).

Children of God

The treasure that the Holy Spirit gives to us in the eucharist is oneness with the family of God. "What we have seen and heard we are telling you so that you too may be in fellowship with us, as we are in union with the Father and with his Son Jesus Christ" (1 Jn 1:3). We are in union with the Trinity because the Holy Spirit is poured out to us through the glorified humanity of Jesus in the eucharist. But that union is effected by the Holy Spirit who raises our human natures to a true sonship and daughtership with the Father by the oneness we enjoy in the eucharist with the only-begotten Son of God. We are truly children of God.

Everyone moved by the Spirit is a son of God. The Spirit you received is not the spirit of slaves bringing fear into your lives again; it is the spirit of sons, and it makes us cry out, "Abba, Father!" The Spirit himself and our spirit bear united witness that we are children of God, and if we are children we are heirs as well: heirs of God and co-heirs with Christ, sharing his sufferings so as to share his glory. (Rm 8:14-17; also, Ga 4:6-7; Jn 14:15-17; 14:26; 15:27; 16:7-11; 16:13-14)

In the eucharist *par excellence* we experience the Father begetting us in his one Son through his Spirit. "You are my son, today I have become your father" (Ps 2:7). In a way, we can say that the Father loves only one person and that is his own Son, Jesus Christ. But he loves us with an infinite love as he loves us in him. What reverence ought to be ours as we open our hearts to the perfect love of Jesus for his Father! What joy should flood us as we experience an infinite love of the Father being generated freshly for us in each eucharistic reception as he loves us in Jesus!

Hilary of Poitiers encourages the communicant, who is joined to the Father through Christ, to press on to greater union with the Father. For "Christ himself is in us by his flesh and we are in him, while all that we are is with him in God."[8]

We are more than merely adopted children of God. As has been pointed out earlier, through contact with the humanity of Christ, the eucharist through the Holy Spirit effects a union between us and God that makes us truly sharers of God's very divine nature. Symeon the New Theologian (+1022) expresses this awesome mystery:

I receive in Communion
the Body divinized as being that of God.
I too become god
in this inexpressible union.
See what a mystery!
The soul then and the body . . .
are one being in two essences.
Therefore these are one and two

in communion with Christ
and drinking his blood,
they are united to two essences,
united in this way to the essences of my God,
    they become god by participation.
They are called by the same name as that of him
in whom they have participated on a level of essence.
They say that coal is fire
and the iron is black.
Yet when the iron is immersed in the fire
it appears as fire.
If it then appears as such,
we also can call it by that name.
We see it as fire,
we can call it fire.[9]

We are received into the only-begotten Son of God by an *ontological* union, a unique oneness with God. Marriage perhaps comes closest to describing such a union and yet even that fails to express the oneness of persons, Trinity and ourselves individually and all of us together united in the eucharist.

M. V. Bernadot, O.P., by means of analogies, strives to describe the intimacy of the communicant and God in this eucharistic union, but such analogies always fail to throw adequate light on this mystery.

As perfume percolates the containing vessel, and the ray the crystal, giving purity and brilliance; like fire permeating iron, warming and enkindling, so Grace from the Eucharist flowing into my soul, possesses, penetrates, fills, in the words of Thomas "transforms and inebriates with God."[10]

Because Jesus Christ through his Spirit takes us up, not only into his human nature, but into his very divine nature, we are more than adopted children. We can say with John: "Think of the love that the Father has lavished on us, by letting us be called God's children; and that is what we are. My dear people, we are already the children of God" (1 Jn 3:1-2).

We in the eucharist experience ourselves more deeply being regenerated by the Father into a oneness with Jesus Christ as his Son. Scheeben is one of the boldest of modern theologians to express this substantial union with Christ received in the eucharist:

> In the Eucharist we receive life from God; and we receive it by substantial union with his Son, inasmuch as we become bone of his bone and flesh of his flesh. Indeed, our substantial connection with him is more enduring than that which exists among men between parent and child. For in this latter case the substantial union ceases with birth; but in the Eucharist it can and should be continually renewed and strengthened. And so in virtue of the Eucharist we not merely receive our life from God, as children do from their earthly parents, but we live in God; we have our life from his substance and in his substance. Eucharistic Communion with God has the double function of begetting and nourishing the children of God.[11]

One with each other

In the eucharist we are not only united with the Trinity, but we attain a new oneness with the others in whom the same trinitarian life lives, especially within the context of the eucharistic celebration. Here is where the Church, the body of Christ, comes together in loving union with its head, Jesus Christ. The liturgy, or the "work" of the people of God, has to be always the context (except in emergencies such as communion given to the sick) in which the eucharist is received. The liturgy is the sacred place and time when the Church is most realized by the power of the Holy Spirit. It is the realization of the life of the Church for which it exists: to praise and glorify God for the gifts of life and salvation we have received.

It is especially in the reception of the eucharist that all members of Christ's body are most powerfully united in a new sense of oneness with each other. They symbolically enter into the depth of the richness of God's self-sacrificing love. The eucharist is not only a sacrament, but it is also the ever-now sacrifice of Christ for us to the Father unto our healing and redemption. It is the culmination of all the sacraments as encounters with Christ in his self-giving to us, for in the eucharist Jesus Christ gives himself as he did in the first eucharistic celebration of the Last Supper before his death and as he did on the cross. He gives himself solemnly to die on our behalf, ratifying by this visible, external ritual act the whole meaning and basic choice of his earthly life. "Now has the Son of Man been glorified, and in him God has been glorified" (Jn 13:21).

All of Christ's other powerful miracles and healings have meaning in the light of this greatest power of communication whereby he gives himself to us in the complete gift. He not merely expresses his desire to die for us individually and communally for the whole of mankind, but he gives us his body as food and his blood as drink. He finds a way to remain among us, imaging always the sacrificing love of the Father unto the last drop of water and blood for us.

In making the first Covenant, Yahweh had promised to be faithful to his people if they would faithfully observe the Torah. He also showed himself the patient, tender spouse of Israel. Jesus renews this tender, spousal love of God for his people. The eucharist is the banquet and Jesus is the bridegroom. The Church, made up of the community of individual believers in him, is the bride. Lives are to be changed. Abiding in the eucharistic union with the Father and the Son, we are to bring forth fruit in abundance. "It is to the glory of my Father that you should bear much fruit, and then you will be my disciples. . . . Remain in my love. If you keep my commandments, you will remain in my love. This is my commandment: love one another as I have loved you" (Jn 15:8-12).

The divinizing power of the Trinity experienced in the eucharist is to be the power that drives us outward toward other communities to be eucharist, bread broken, to give ourselves, not only as Jesus did on our behalf, but with Jesus and the Father abiding within us with their Spirit of love empowering us to do that which would be impossible for us alone to do consistently. Paul sees immediately the application of the eucharist-community to the Christian family. "Husbands should love their wives just as Christ loved the Church and sacrificed himself for her to make her holy" (Eph 5:25).

Remission of sin

The sacrifice of Jesus Christ acted out in the eucharistic liturgy is unto the remission of our sins. This is not a legalistic *quid pro quo* contract to satisfy the demands of divine justice. The blood of Jesus that remits our sins and heals us unto eternal life is to be a daily experience of the depths of God's love manifested to us by Jesus' complete self-giving. His ardent love, experienced in the eucharist, is a reliving of the same dynamic, *ever-now* love of Jesus, God-man, for us as he touches us with both his humanity and divinity and takes away the condition of sin in our lives. Loved so by God the Father, Son and Holy Spirit, we need no longer resort to sinful actions, words and thoughts that are egocentered and destructive of community oneness. We can, by the power of the Holy Spirit, who reveals to us, within these symbols of food and drink, the presence of the loving Trinity, let go of our lives and live and love as God does.

The Church, as a community of one body united in love to the one head, Jesus Christ, is formed out of the womb of Christ's heart that is an image of the heart of the Father. Water and blood, two elements that John sees at the foot of the cross (Jn 19:34), are to be symbols of the creative forces of the female, symbols of the life-giving power that Jesus, dying on the cross, gives to his bride, the Church, signs of the birth-giving waters of baptism and the nourishing body and blood of Christ in the eucharist. John Chrysostom comments on the wounded side of Christ.

> The lance of the soldier opened the side of Christ, and behold . . . from his wounded side Christ built the Church, as once the first mother, Eve, was formed from Adam. Hence Paul says: Of his flesh we are and of his bone. By that he means the wounded side of Jesus. As God took the rib out of Adam's side and from it formed the woman, so Christ gives us water and blood from his wounded side and forms from it the Church . . . there the slumber of Adam; here the death-sleep of Jesus.[12]

We are born spiritually as God's children, brothers and sisters to each other as we truly live the sacrament of baptism that reaches its fullness of loving union between us and God and between one another of us human brothers and sisters in the eucharist. In the Old Covenant the blood of goats and bulls and the ashes of heifers were sprinkled on those who incurred defilement and they were restored to the holiness of their outward lives. "How much more effectively the blood of Christ, who offered himself as the perfect sacrifice to God through the eternal Spirit, can purify our inner self from dead actions so that we do our service to the living God" (Heb 9:13-14).

Self-sacrifice

Through his humanity, his body and blood, Jesus Christ is the victim, but in the eucharist we also receive the only existing Jesus Christ, glorified and spiritualized by the victory of resurrection over sin and death. We are to draw strength from this sacrifice to stir us also to sacrifice ourselves for each other. We are to participate in Christ's sacrifice by offering ourselves, not only to God, but concretely we are to be consumed by the fire of love of God in Jesus Christ through his Spirit to go forth and be a living sacrifice of love to all that we meet.

The principal fruit of the eucharist, "the communion in the Holy Spirit," is an intimate union of all in the mystical body of Christ. We find in the *epiklesis* of Basil's liturgy the stress on this union: "So that all who participate from one bread may be made one by the action of the Spirit." This is the central scope of the eucharist, the union of all the faithful through the mutual union of each individual with the Holy Trinity. The eucharist creates the unity of all who participate in the same holy bread.

This comes through a single effusion of the Holy Spirit in all the communicants who receive the bread of life with sincerity and fervor. Paul tells us that it is the Holy Spirit who pours out gifts in order to "edify" or build up the body of Christ, the Church. "There is a variety of gifts but always the same Spirit; there are all sorts of services to be done, but always to the same Lord" (1 Co 12:4-5). Again Paul writes: "There is one body, one Spirit, just as you were all called into one and the same hope when you were called. There is one Lord, one faith, one baptism, and one God who is Father of all, over all, through all and within all" (Eph 4:4-6).

Therefore, we not only receive Jesus Christ in the eucharist in order to praise God the Father and surrender ourselves to him in the same self-surrendering act of Jesus Christ on the cross, but we are to be transformed interiorly by Christ's Spirit. "Be renewed in the spirit of your mind" (Eph 4:23). By praising and glorifying the heavenly Father, we open ourselves in the eucharist and at all times after the eucharist to his transforming blessing that he breathes upon us to make us a true, effective, eucharistic blessing to all whom we meet.

We put on the mind of Christ in the eucharist when we face with him a broken, suffering world. We become a living part of the body of Christ, we become Church when we share the caring love of Jesus for each suffering person we meet. Pain gnaws at our hearts as we suffer the pain of the heart of Christ not to be able to do more for the poor and afflicted in all parts of the world. We suffer in our own inadequacies that do not allow us to know what we can effectively do to alleviate the physical and moral evils rampant in the world.

With Paul we can ask whether we have received Christ's body in the eucharist if, after the liturgical celebration, we do not receive, as a brother or sister of our one Father, each human being who enters our life.

> And so anyone who eats the bread or drinks the cup of the Lord unworthy will be behaving unworthily towards the body and blood of the Lord . . . because a person who eats and drinks without recognizing the body is eating and drinking his own condemnation. (1 Co 11:27-29)

Paul was speaking about sins against charity toward fellow Christians. He had earlier in the same epistle commented on the oneness that true reception of the body of Jesus Christ effects. "The fact that there is only one loaf means that, though there are many of us, we form a single body, because we all have share in this one loaf" (1 Co 10:17).

The eucharist is not fully received unless it is lived. And the living eucharist is our daily life in Jesus Christ where we live no longer we ourselves, but he truly lives in us (Ga 2:20).

We are to go out and to be eucharist to every man, woman and child that God sends into our lives. What a tremendous responsibility for Christians who believe the doctrine of the eucharist and receive this gift of gifts even daily! Our eucharistic life is to be measured by the fruit of the Spirit that is love, peace, joy, gentleness, kindliness, patience and forbearance (Ga 5:22). We are to "bear with one another charitably, in complete selflessness, gentleness and patience. Do all you can to preserve the unity of the Spirit by the peace that binds you together" (Eph 4:2).

We are to use our special charisms or gifts given us by the Holy Spirit to build up the body of Christ. If one part of the body of Christ is wounded or sick, the healthy parts come to the aid of the injured member. But the greatest sign of whether we have truly received the full body of Christ is measured by love, for this is the indication of how much of God's eucharistic love has been received in receiving the body and blood of Jesus Christ, the image of the Father. Such love is toward others as Jesus, the imaged love of the Father, was always toward others in loving service. "If I, then, the Lord and Master, have washed your feet, you should wash each other's feet" (Jn 13:14). This eucharistic love is always patient and kind, never jealous, never boastful or conceited, never rude or selfish. It does not take offense and is not resentful. It takes no pleasure in other people's sins but delights in the truth. It is always ready to excuse, to trust, to hope and to endure whatever comes (1 Co 13:4-6).

The cosmic eucharist

The fruit of the eucharist as the gift of the Holy Spirit unifying us who have received Jesus Christ in love with all mankind is beautifully described by Teilhard de Chardin:

> The gift you ask of me for these brothers of mine—the only gift my heart can give—is not the overflowing tenderness of those special, preferential loves which you implant in our lives as the most powerful created agent of our inward growth; it is something less tender but just as real and of even greater strength. Your will is that, with the help of your Eucharist, between men and my

brother-men there should be revealed that basic attraction (already dimly felt in every love once it becomes strong) which mystically transforms the myriads of rational creatures into (as it were) a single monad in you, Christ Jesus.[13]

Jesus, the risen Lord over all the universe, the *Pantocrator,* by his resurrection is inserted as a leaven inside of the entire, material cosmos. Yet he operates, he speaks, he touches, he loves the poor and the destitute.

He conquers sin and death empirically only through his living members. Those who worthily have received his body and blood and have received the outpoured Holy Spirit in the eucharist are to go out and celebrate the eucharistic liturgy of the high-priest, Jesus Christ. God truly loves the world he created. He looked upon it and saw it to be very good (Gn 1:18). He has created all things, every atom of matter, in and through his Word, Jesus Christ. We are to go forth from the altar of the Lord to witness to the sustaining presence of God's Logos, not only living within us, but also sustaining all of creation. Having received the Trinity and having been divinized into their very community of one in unity and many in self-giving relationships, we are to go forth and draw out these energies of the same Trinity that bathe the whole universe and charge it with God's infinite love.

Eucharistic ministries

The body of Christ is being formed through the eucharistic ministry of each human being made according to that image and likeness that is Jesus Christ. That body of Christ is being shaped and fashioned by all things material. There are prophets of doom who point out the chaotic confusion and dogmatically declare as Sartre did that life has "no exit." Nevertheless Christians, who have eaten the bread of life, point to the inner, loving presence of the cosmic Christ within matter, within this crazy, careening world. They show that there is a divine purpose, similar to the purpose revealed to them as they reverently received the glorified humanity of Jesus Christ. The same Holy Spirit that swept them and their fellow communicants into a realized oneness with Jesus Christ and his Father reveals to them at each step of their lives how to effect that same union with the world. The Spirit reveals the inner presence, now being activated in time and place by the persons in whom Jesus Christ lives, of that same Jesus Christ as he evolves the universe into his body. He is moving it toward *Omega* which he is. "I am the Alpha and the Omega, says the Lord God, who is, who was, and who is to come, the Almighty" (Rv 1:8).

Such "eucharized" Christians live in the vision of the dynamic love energies inside of the material world. They can call other people to their awesome dignity of cooperating with these uncreated energies of God. Creation is not finished. The cosmic liturgy has not yet reached communion, men and women, united with each other as brothers and sisters of Jesus Christ and of the one heavenly Father, human beings in peace and harmony with the sub-human cosmos, bringing it into fulfillment according to God's eternal plan. They have entered through the eucharist into a life in Christ, a new creation. The old communion for them has gone, and now the new one is here.

> It is all God's Work. It was God who reconciled us to himself through Christ and gave us the work of handing on this reconciliation. In other words, God in Christ was reconciling the world to himself not holding men's faults against them, and he has entrusted to us the news that they are reconciled. (2 Co 5:18-19)

As men and women work, ever more conscious of the indwelling Trinity brought to such a peak of experience in the eucharist, they join the gifts of creativity placed within them by God's graces with the working power of the triune God, Father, Son and Holy Spirit. In humility they can also see the pruning hand of God, the divine pedagogue, as he instructs his children, corrects, admonishes, exhorts them in what seems to be, for those not in the body of Christ, at times, sheer negative evil, physical or moral.

They live each moment in the resurrectional hope that is engendered in the social and historical horizontal. Instead of running away from involvement in the activities of this world, such Christians move to the "inside" presence of the Trinity at the heart of matter. What any human being adds to make this world a better world in Christ Jesus has an eternal effect on the whole process. When the love experienced in the eucharist becomes the dominant force in the lives of such Christians, then every thought, word and deed is bathed in the light of the indwelling Trinity inside the whole world.

Thus the building up of the body of Christ, the Church, is not the gathering of an elite group out of the human race, while the rest of creation is destined for destruction. It is to be the resurrected body of God's creation, evolving through history and brought to its completion with our cooperation. The only obstacles that hold back the process are the same that do not allow us truly to receive the body of Christ fully in the eucharist: the evils of selfishness, fear and pride.

Conclusion

In his introduction to the works of William Blake, the poet Yeats wrote: "We perceive the world through countless little reflections of our own image."[14] We spend most of our lives creating the world according to our own needs. Religious leaders often easily help in this process as they encourage their "faithful" to build their own world and in that man-created world they are to know that they have been saved. But the entire Christian revelation consists in the power of Jesus Christ as light, coming into our darkened world, and leading us through his Spirit to the source of all reality, the heavenly Father.

He is the image of the Father and we have been made according to his likeness (Gn 1:26). Jesus Christ has taken upon himself our human nature in order to set us free from our illusions and false worlds. He came to reveal that all reality, all of our created world, has come out of the family of God, a tri-unity of three persons in one nature. Creation is an ongoing presence of God as one energizing love, touching our world with three personalized relations of fatherhood, sonship and spiration of love.

This unity in Trinity, the motionless movement of God toward his world as the receptacle of his love, becomes manifested to us when God's Logos, the Son of the Father, assumed flesh in the mystery of the incarnation. Now through the humanity of Jesus Christ God the Trinity touches us and through us touches the material world. Through his death and resurrection, Jesus Christ is able to send us God's Spirit. It is in the eucharist, as we have seen, that we reach the climax of these two mysteries that bring us into true reality, that of the Trinity and the incarnation.

We are called to live in this reality of the all-pervasive, loving presence of the Trinity acting through the mediation of the God-man, Jesus Christ. This is what a Christian mystic really is. As we celebrate the divine liturgy, our faith makes us vividly aware of this trinitarian presence, when, in microcosmic fashion, Jesus the high-priest breathes over a small segment of the Church, including the gifts of bread and wine, and his Spirit of love transfigures that part of the incomplete world into a sharing in Christ's divine nature. The authentic Christian mystic extends this transfiguring liturgy throughout the day in every thought, word and deed, done for God's glory. No matter how insignificant, banal and monotonous our work may be, we are to be vibrantly aware of Jesus Christ, already glorified, living within us and working through us to bring the whole world to its fullness.

As communion with the body and blood of Jesus Christ brings the contemplative Christian into the dynamic presence of the Trinity, so this communion with his is extended into the materiality of each day. The false division between the profane and the sacred ceases as we prayfully contemplate the Holy Trinity in all of creation. Contemplation flows from the fullness of our activities, because we find the Trinity in the very activity of the moment. We discover the divine richness in the most commonplace action. We find the Holy Trinity at work for the redemption of the human race and we become an instrument of applying that divine, healing love to each person we meet. We have new "eyes" with which to see, not only the uncreated energies of the one God, essentially working out of love, but to see also and to experience the divine Father becoming our Father and the Father of all our brothers and sisters. We see the Son, not only always adoring the Father in total self-surrendering love, but we see him also as our head, while we are parts and members of his total, complete body. We experience the loving presence of the Spirit, not only binding the Father and Son into a oneness that calls out their uniqueness of persons, but also binding ourselves and all other human beings and the whole material universe into a oneness of the body of Christ with a uniqueness assigned to each individual human person and each material creature.

A modern contemplative

For such a contemplative, there is no insignificant event that does not bear the stamp of the Holy Trinity's actively involved, loving presence, touching the world through the humanity of Jesus Christ, now joined to that of the person of prayer in order to bring it to completion according to the original plan as conceived by the Holy Trinity. Such a contemplative patiently lives day by day in the mystery of the Trinity's presence in life. We shun any objectivizing of this awesome mystery of God as one and God as three loving relationships to each other and to ourselves.

We are humble pilgrims always searching deeper into reality that is permeated by the triune presence of Father, Son and Holy Spirit. We cry out for pardon and cleansing: "Lord, Jesus Christ, Son of God, have mercy on me a sinner!" We approach each moment as we do the moment in the divine liturgy when we are about to receive the fiery coal of divine love in the eucharist: "Approach with faith and in the fear of God." The mystery of the Trinity does not mean that we cannot experience the reality of God's loving *we*-community. It means that such knowledge is beyond our human acquisition, but it is given to those who hunger and thirst for it. Paul believed that such knowledge was available to the poor of spirit:

> Out of his infinite glory, may he give you the power through his Spirit for your hidden self to grow strong, so that Christ may live in your hearts through faith, and then, planted in love and built on love, you will with all the saints have strength to grasp the breadth and the length, the height and the depth; until, knowing the love of Christ, which is beyond all knowledge, you are filled with the utter fullness of God. (Eph 3:16-19)

God is a fullness, an inexhaustible source of love that seeks continuously to share his very being with us human beings. But he seeks to reveal himself as Trinity and as One to those who move beyond the type of *religion* that allows us to fashion our own images of God and of the world and of others after our own image. To the little ones of this earth, the poor of spirit and clean of heart, God reveals through his Holy Spirit how simple bread and wine can open us up to the living bread of life, Jesus Christ, true God and true man. The eucharistic Lord leads us to the ever-present Father of both Jesus Christ and of ourselves who through the eucharist have become united one with the only-begotten Son of God. Through the eucharist such little ones move into the world and find the presence of the risen Jesus, not only in bread and wine, but in the little pebble, the smile of a child, the sparkle in the wise eyes of an old man. The whole world is a part of the eternal liturgy that the Lamb of God is offering to the heavenly Father. The heart of all reality is eucharist: receiving God's great love for us in his Son incarnated, Jesus Christ, through the illumination of the Holy Spirit who empowers us to return that love in self-surrendering service to each person we meet. The Trinity is at the beginning of all reality and it is there that we end up in humble adoration.

T. S. Eliot, in his *Four Quartets,* well describes our search for the utter fullness of God:

> We shall not cease from exploration,
> And the end of all our exploring
>   Will be to arrive where we started
> And know the place for the first time.[15]

A fitting conclusion to such a book for an author who has striven to present the apophatic side of the mystery of the Trinity and yet has succeeded in the process to write so many pages are the words of Symeon the New Theologian (+1022) who will recall us to this awesome mystery that can be perceived only by the humble and meek of heart.

> So then come and place yourself with us, O my brother,
> on the mountain of divine knowledge of divine contemplation
> and together let us hear the Father's voice—O alas!
> How far are we from the divine dignity!

How far away are we from eternal life!
How far or even farther are we all, really,
from the dignity of God and divine contemplation,
even if we should affirm in a contradictory way that we
    abide in him
and we possess in us him who abides in unapproachable
    light,
who also entirely remains and abides in us,
and yet we would wish, seated in the bowels of
    the earth,
to philosophize on things that transcend this earth,
on things of heaven and even higher things than that,
    as though we saw reality accurately,
and so we seek to explain to everyone and enjoy being
    called learned men,
theologians, experts and mystics of divine secrets
which just proves completely our stupidity.
    . . . But, O my Christ, deliver those who are tied to you
from the unclean vanity and pride.
Make us participators in your sufferings and your glory
and deign to make us never to be separated from you,
now and in the future world to come,
forever and ever. Amen.[16]

Notes

1. Monika Hellwig, *The Eucharist and the Hunger of the World* (New York, 1975), 42.
2. Gregory of Nyssa, *De Oratione Catech. Magna* 37 (*LNPF*, 2d Series, 5:504-505).
3. *Ibid.,* 506.
4. John Chrysostom, *Homilies on St. John's Gospel,* trans. Sr. Thomas Aquinas Goggin, S.C.H. in *Fathers of the Church* (New York: Fathers of the Church, Inc., 1957), 33:468-69.
5. An excellent treatment of the doctrine of Cyril of Alexandria on the image and

likeness is found in W. Burghardt, *The Image of God in Man According to Cyril of Alexandria* (Washington: Catholic University of America Press, 1957).

6. Cyril of Alexandria, *Commentary on St. John's Gospel (PG* 74:553-561).
7. The Liturgies of Basil and John Chrysostom.
8. Hilary of Poitiers, *De Trinitate* 15 *(PL,* 42:248).
9. Symeon the New Theologian, *Hymns,* 30.169-70.
10. M.V. Bernadot, O.P., *From Holy Communion to the Blessed Trinity* (Westminster: The Newman Bookshop, 1947), 44.
11. M. Scheeben, *The Mysteries of Christianity,* trans. Cyril Vollert, S.J. (St. Louis: B. Herder Book Co., 1946) 493-94.
12. Cited by Hugo Rahner, S.J., "The Beginnings of the Devotion in Patristic Times," in *Heart of the Savior,* ed. Josef Stierli (New York: Herder & Herder, 1957), 54.
13. Teilhard de Chardin, *Hymn of the Universe* (New York: Harper & Row, 1965), 92.
14. William Butler Yeats and E. J. Ellis, eds., *The Works of William Blake* (London, 1893), 1:276.
15. T.S. Eliot, *Four Quartets* (New York: Harcourt & Brace & Co., 1943), 39.
16. Symeon the New Theologian, *Hymns,* 52.265-66.

Select Bibliography

Books:

Augustine. *The Trinity.* Translated by Edmund Hill, The Works of Saint Augustine, vol. I/5. New York: New City Press, 1991.

Congar, Yves. *I Believe in the Holy Spirit.* 3 vols. Translated by David Smith. New York: The Seabury Press, 1983; London: Geoffrey Chapman Co., 1983.

De Regnon, T. *Etudes de théologie positive sur la S. Trinité.* 3 vols. Paris: Aubier, 1892-98.

Fransen, Piet. *Divine Grace and Man.* New York: Desclée Co., 1962.

Hilary of Poitiers. *The Trinity.* Translated by Stephen McKenna, The Fathers of the Church Series, vol. 25. Washington: Catholic University Press, 1954.

Hill, William. *Proper Relations to the Indwelling Divine Persons.* Washington: The Thomist Press, 1956.

Lossky, Vladimir. *The Mystical Theology of the Eastern Church.* London: James Clarke & Co., 1957.

_____. *In the Image and Likeness of God.* New York: St. Vladimir Press, 1974.

Maloney, George A. *Invaded by God: Mysticism and the Indwelling Trinity.* Denville: Dimension Books, 1979.

_____. *A Theology of Uncreated Energies.* Milwaukee: Marquette University Press, 1978.

Mühlen, Heribert. *Der Heilige Geist als Person.* Münster: Aschendorff, 1966.

Pannikkar, Raimundo. *The Trinity and the Religious Experience of Man.* New York: Orbis Books, 1973.

Rahner, Karl. *The Trinity.* Translated by Joseph Donceel. New York: Herder & Herder, 1969.

_____. *Nature and Grace.* Translated by Dinah Wharton. London: Sheed & Ward, 1963.

Sheeben, M. J. *The Mysteries of Christianity.* Translated by Cyril Vollert. St. Louis: B. Herder Book Co., 1946.

Symeon the New Theologian. *Hymns of Divine Love.* Translated by George A. Maloney. Denville: Dimension Books, 1975.

Articles:

Brocken, J. "The Holy Trinity as a Community of Divine Persons." *Heythrop Journal* 15 (1975): 166-82; 257-70.

Cousins, Ewert. "A Theology of Interpersonal Relations." *Thought* 45 (1970): 56-82.

O'Connell, T. "Grace, Relationship and Transcendental Analysis." *Thought* 48 (1973): 360-85.